GCSE

Oxford Literature Companions

Lord of the Flies

WILLIAM GOLDING

WORKBOOK

Notes and activities: Jane Branson
Series consultant: Peter Buckroyd

OXFORD
UNIVERSITY PRESS

Contents

Introduction

What are Oxford Literature Companions?

Oxford Literature Companions is a series designed to provide you with comprehensive support for popular set texts. You can use the Companion workbook alongside your novel, using relevant sections during your studies or using the workbook as a whole for revision. The workbook will help you to create your own personalized guide to the text.

What are the main features within this workbook?

Each workbook in the Oxford Literature Companion series follows the same approach and includes the following features:

Activities

Each workbook offers a range of varied and in-depth activities to deepen understanding and encourage close work with the text, covering characters, themes, language and context. The Skills and Practice chapter also offers advice on assessment and includes sample questions and student answers. There are spaces to write your answers throughout the workbook.

Key terms and quotations

Throughout the workbook, key terms are highlighted in the text and explained on the same page. There is also a detailed glossary at the end of the workbook that explains, in the context of the novel, all the relevant literary terms highlighted.

Quotations from the novel appear in blue text throughout this workbook.

Upgrade

As well as providing guidance on key areas of the novel, throughout this workbook you will also find 'Upgrade' features. These are tips to help with your exam preparation and performance.

Progress check

Each chapter of the workbook ends with a 'Progress check'. Through self-assessment, these enable you to establish how confident you feel about what you have been learning and help you to set next steps and targets.

Which edition of the novel has this workbook used?

Quotations have been taken from the Faber & Faber edition of *Lord of the Flies* (ISBN 978-0571191475).

Plot and structure

Understanding plot

Although you are reading *Lord of the Flies* because you are going to be examined on it, it is important to think about how and why William Golding set out to write this story. Ideally, read the whole book all the way through for enjoyment – and then start rereading, for study purposes.

> **plot** the main events of a play, novel, film, or similar work, presented by the writer as an interrelated sequence

Activity 1

Keep a reading log. Start your reading log below and continue on separate paper. Add a few lines of notes every time you read, to keep track of main events and your feelings and reactions to **plot** events and characters. Here is an example to get you started:

Pages read	What's happening	My thoughts and feelings
Beginning of Chapter 1	A plane has crashed (after being attacked) on an island – seems uninhabited. It's very hot and exotic. Two boys introduced – Ralph and Piggy. They talk, find a conch shell and Ralph blows it.	We see Ralph first but hear Piggy first – probably important. R is excited – 'laughed delightedly... and stood on his head' – and a bit mean to Piggy, who is fat and an orphan ("Sucks to your ass-mar!"). Ralph seems to be in charge already – he blows on the conch even though Piggy knows what it is.

Upgrade

Notice that this student is already beginning to incorporate short quotations into their notes. You should do this too – it will help you to become more familiar with the text. Knowing a number of short quotations from throughout the novel will help you to feel confident in the exam and you will be able to embed them easily in your written answers.

The island

In *Lord of the Flies*, the island setting is closely related to plot, because the boys make such an impact on the island and the boys' environment has a huge effect on them. The different parts of the island and the way they are used and represented as the story develops are important.

Activity 2

Draw a sketch of the island. You should label it with the landmarks that you learn about as you read on, but here are a few to get you started:

- 'the scar' – site of the plane crash • the lagoon where Ralph first swims
- the highest point of the island • the meeting platform • the beach.

Upgrade

Make your map an even more useful revision tool by copying it onto separate paper, and adding quotations and notes about the places and the events that happen in them as you make your way through the text.

Key quotation

Jack pointed down.

"That's where we landed."

Beyond falls and cliffs there was a gash visible in the trees; there were the splintered trunks and then the drag, leaving only a fringe of palm between the scar and the sea.

(Chapter 1)

Keeping track

Keeping track of the action is important: by the time you get to the exam, you will want to have strong recall of all the major scenes and events in the story. Your reading log will help, as will the next activity.

Activity 3

Here is a list of some of the main events in the novel out of sequence. Reorder the list correctly to show that you can recall the key events in the right order as they happen in the text.

A plane crashes on a tropical island. ☐

Simon sees the dead parachutist and runs to tell everyone it's not a beast. ☐

The first successful pig hunt. ☐

Piggy is killed. ☐

The boy with the mulberry birthmark goes missing. ☐

Jack's gang tries to smoke Ralph out of his hiding place. ☐

Ralph is elected leader. ☐

Sam and Eric see what they think is a beast on the mountain. ☐

Jack's gang steals Piggy's glasses. ☐

Simon is murdered. ☐

Ralph and Piggy find the conch. ☐

A ship is seen. ☐

Understanding structure

> **structure** the way a text develops across its parts

Tracking patterns in a text is another good way to understand how its plot works and draws your attention to **structure** too.

Activity 4

a) Copy the table below onto separate paper. Reread the final one or two paragraphs of each chapter and decide how tense or dramatic things are at these points. Rate the tension with a score out of 10 and give brief reasons for your thinking, as in the example.

Chapter	Key quotation	Tension score	Reasons
1	'Next time there would be no mercy.'	6	Sinister hint at future violence
2	'drum-roll' on the 'unfriendly side of the mountain'	7	Sounds like the island is going to 'fight back'
3			

b) Transfer your tension evaluations onto a graph. The line you draw to connect all the plot points will be an indication of where tension rises and drama increases across the novel.

c) Pick out what you think are two key moments of high tension. Make notes for each about the effect on the reader in those moments and why you think Golding wanted the tension to be high at these points.

To understand plot fully we must take notice of tiny details as well as major episodes or events, so sometimes we need to read more carefully and closely. The characteristics of stronger and weaker responses to plot are shown below.

Strong answers	Weak answers
Main events of plot referred to and important details picked out.	Show knowledge of main events.
Range of comments about how plot links to other aspects of the novel, such as character development.	Limited comments about how plot links to other aspects of the novel, such as character development.
Students focus on what the events mean or suggest, using expressions like 'hints at', 'underlines', 'emphasizes' and 'making the reader wonder' to explore less obvious meanings.	Students just retell the story using their own words.

Activity 5

Look below at the two student answers to the question 'How does Golding use events in this extract from Chapter 8 to explore Simon's character?'

Use the table about strong and weak answers, on page 7, to help you annotate the two answers as if you are the teacher, explaining the strengths and weaknesses of each, and giving advice on improvements if they are needed.

> Simon looked up, feeling the weight of his wet hair, and gazed at the sky. Up there, for once, were clouds, great bulging towers that sprouted away over the island, grey and cream and copper-coloured. The clouds were sitting on the land; they squeezed, produced moment by moment, this close, tormenting heat. Even the butterflies deserted the open space where the obscene thing grinned and dripped. Simon lowered his head, carefully keeping his eyes shut, then sheltered them with his hand. There were no shadows under the trees but everywhere a pearly stillness, so that what was real seemed illusive and without definition. The pile of guts was a black blob of flies that buzzed like a saw. After a while these flies found Simon. Gorged, they alighted by his runnels of sweat and drank. They tickled under his nostrils and played leapfrog on his thighs. They were black and iridescent green and without number; and in front of Simon, the Lord of the Flies hung on his stick and grinned. At last Simon gave up and looked back; saw the white teeth and dim eyes, the blood—and his gaze was held by that ancient, inescapable recognition. In Simon's right temple, a pulse began to beat on the brain. (*Chapter 8*)

Student A

> While Ralph and Piggy and their group build a fire near the meeting platform and Jack establishes his hunters as a new gang, Simon has slipped away. He is sitting, all sweaty, surrounded by flies, in a secret, jungly part of the island, looking at the pig's head on a stick. He shades his eyes at first but eventually looks up and stares at the pig's head.

Student B

> Once again, Simon is shown to be an outsider, as he doesn't join in with building the new fire or with Jack's new hunter group. The unusual stormy clouds give a hint of menace and tell us something strange is happening, and the lack of butterflies underlines the sinister mood. At first, Simon cannot bear to look at the pig's head but the connection between them is emphasized by the flies that move on to drink Simon's sweat. Eventually, he looks up and experiences a moment of 'inescapable recognition', making the reader wonder about the link between them. Is Simon sympathizing with the Lord of the Flies, because he's a victim too, or is he recognizing something else they have in common?

Activity 6

a) Read the extract from Chapter 11 below, which describes the death of Piggy. Write your own comments on it using the prompts provided. Do not just retell the story – focus on suggesting what the events mean.

> The rock struck Piggy a glancing blow from chin to knee; the conch exploded into a thousand white fragments and ceased to exist. Piggy, saying nothing, with no time for even a grunt, travelled through the air sideways from the rock, turning over as he went. The rock bounded twice and was lost in the forest. Piggy fell forty feet and landed on his back across that square, red rock in the sea. His head opened and stuff came out and turned red. Piggy's arms and legs twitched a bit, like a pig's after it has been killed. Then the sea breathed again in a long slow sigh, the water boiled white and pink over the rock; and when it went, sucking back again, the body of Piggy was gone.
> (*Chapter 11*)

i. The simultaneous destruction of Piggy and the conch…

----

ii. The comparison of Piggy to a pig 'after it has been killed'…

----

iii. The rock that is 'lost in the forest' and the sighing sea…

----

b) Now try this activity again. This time do it without prompts and choose your own extract to comment on. For example, you might select the description of the first fire-making (Chapter 2) or the penultimate paragraph of the novel, when Ralph breaks down in front of the naval officer (Chapter 12).

Activity 7

Read back what you have written about the extract you chose in Activity 6b and ask yourself the following questions:

- Have you done more than retell the story? ☐

- Have you suggested what the events or actions might mean? ☐

- Have you used any words or phrases to suggest less obvious meanings? ☐

- Do you need to make any amendments or try again? ☐

Linking events

At the beginning of this chapter we focused on the plot as a sequence of **chronologically** told events. However, to do well in your exam you also need to be able to make links across the text to show how different events, objects, characters and places might be connected. One way to do this is by creating a spider diagram to show the links.

> **chronologically** in time order, beginning with the earliest

Activity 8

Complete the spider diagram for the conch, extending what has been started below with details from Chapter 5 onwards. Add notes, quotations and extra lines to show how the points connect.

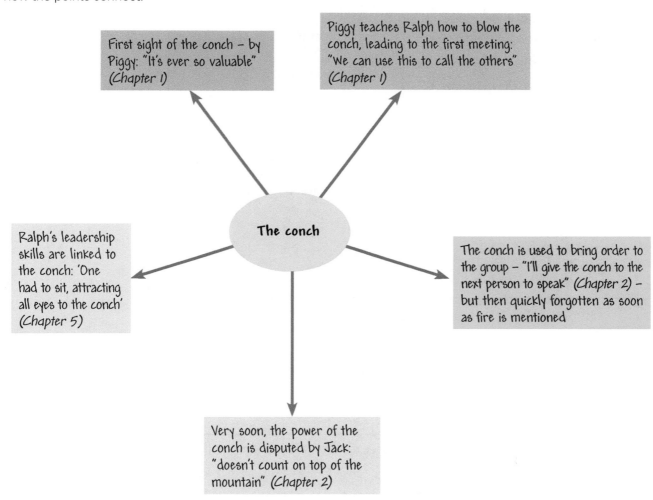

First sight of the conch – by Piggy: "It's ever so valuable" (Chapter 1)

Piggy teaches Ralph how to blow the conch, leading to the first meeting: "We can use this to call the others" (Chapter 1)

Ralph's leadership skills are linked to the conch: 'One had to sit, attracting all eyes to the conch' (Chapter 5)

The conch

The conch is used to bring order to the group – "I'll give the conch to the next person to speak" (Chapter 2) – but then quickly forgotten as soon as fire is mentioned

Very soon, the power of the conch is disputed by Jack: "doesn't count on top of the mountain" (Chapter 2)

Spider diagrams are great for revision. Using the conch spider diagram as an example, make one for:

- all Simon's scenes
- the 'beast'
- Jack and Ralph's relationship
- Piggy.

Foreshadowing

Making spider diagrams will probably draw your attention to how certain events relate to each other. This structural feature is called **foreshadowing**. Golding makes very effective use of it to draw our attention to important themes, to set up tension and to create ominous clues about future events.

Activity 9

Complete the table below to show which events (from early in the novel) foreshadow other, later events. You may need to include more than one event in the first column, as in the example that has been completed.

Early events that foreshadow...	... later events
The first attempt to kill a pig (Chapter 1) Jack's solo hunting attempt (Chapter 3) The first successful pig-killing (Chapter 4)	Simon's death at the hands of the hunters (Chapter 9)
	Simon understanding that the 'beast' is part of the boys' human nature (Chapter 5)
	The attempt to burn Ralph out of the forest (Chapter 12)
	Piggy's murder by Roger (Chapter 11)

Key quotation

Now the fire was nearer; those volleying shots were great limbs, trunks even, bursting. The fools! The fire must be almost at the fruit trees – what would they eat tomorrow? (*Chapter 12*)

Beginnings and endings

Beginnings and endings are usually important when exploring plot and structure.

Activity 10

Answer the following questions.

a) What is the setting of the beginning and end of the novel? Explain why you think Golding might have organized it this way.

----

b) Read these descriptions of Ralph from the beginning and the end of the novel. What do they suggest about how Golding has developed Ralph as a character throughout the novel?

Beginning	End
'stood on his head and grinned' (Chapter 1)	'The tears began to flow and sobs shook him' (Chapter 12)
'his grey shirt stuck to him' (Chapter 1)	'filthy body, matted hair, and unwiped nose' (Chapter 12)
'mildness about his mouth and eyes' (Chapter 1)	'screaming, snarling, bloody' (Chapter 12)

----

c) Using short quotations to support your answer, comment on how the island has changed between the beginning and the end of the novel.

----

d) Compare the first mention of Jack, when he comes along the beach in Chapter 1 as part of 'the creature', to the final description of him as a **'a little boy who wore the remains of an extraordinary black cap on his red hair'**.

Picturing the text

Picturing the text as a shape on the page is one helpful way to understand how it is structured. For example, some stories have a simple beginning–middle–end structure: you could represent this with a three-part flow diagram. A more complicated novel may have many twists and turns, or stories within stories. Many people have argued that *Lord of the Flies* can be read as a traditional **tragedy**, a narrative structure that dates back to Aristotle.

Activity 11

Annotate the diagram of a five-act tragedy below with the events of the novel.

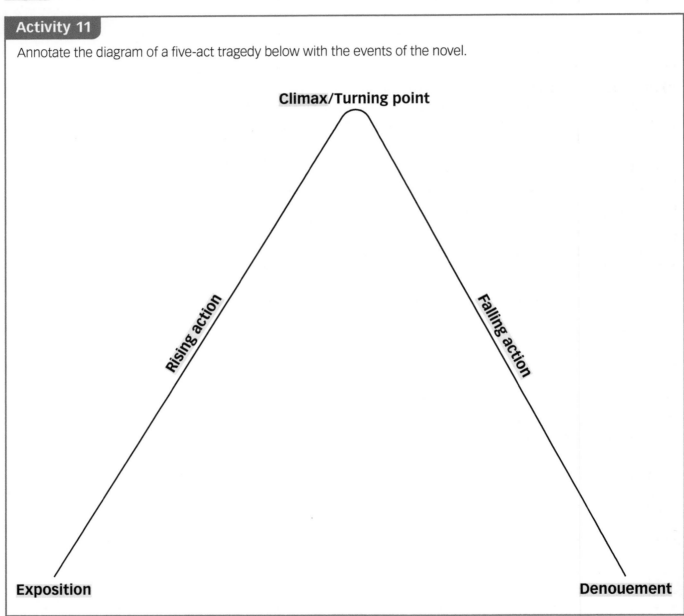

Climax/Turning point

Rising action

Falling action

Exposition

Denouement

climax a significant moment when things go wrong

denouement the final part of a novel when the various strands of the plot are brought together and resolved

exposition an introduction where the scene is set for the drama to follow

falling action when the conflict starts to be resolved but there is continued drama or suspense

rising action a series of problems or conflicts that increase the tension

tragedy a traditional story type with five main stages, first defined by the Ancient Greek philosopher and scientist Aristotle

Activity 12

Here are some other ingredients of a traditional tragedy. Using this information
and the tragedy curve diagram that you have annotated in Activity 11, answer the
question that follows. Continue on separate paper if you need to.

- A tragedy features a hero of high status.
- The hero has a flaw in his character.
- There is some reversal or change of fortunes.

- The hero dies or suffers.
- The hero realizes his flaw too late.
- The audience feel pity/fear.

> To what extent do you think *Lord of the Flies* is a traditional tragedy? Use
> short quotations and detailed reasons to justify your answer.

Progress check

Use the chart below to review the skills you have developed in this chapter.
For each column, start at the bottom box and work your way up towards the
highest level in the top box. Tick the box to show you have achieved that level.

I can sustain a critical response to *Lord of the Flies* and interpret the plot and structure convincingly ☐	I can analyse the effects of Golding's use of language, structure and form in *Lord of the Flies*, using subject terms judiciously ☐
I can develop a coherent response to *Lord of the Flies* and explain the plot and structure clearly ☐	I can explain how Golding uses language, structure and form to create effects in *Lord of the Flies*, using relevant subject terms ☐
I can make some comments on the plot and structure in *Lord of the Flies* ☐	I can identify some of Golding's methods in *Lord of the Flies* and use some subject terms ☐
Personal response	**Language, structure, form**

Context

Understanding context

The **context** of any piece of art can be taken into account to help understand it. In literature, context might include any of the following:

- when a text was written
- events that were happening around the time the text was written and how these may have influenced the writing
- the life experiences of the person who wrote the text and whether these are relevant to the writing
- other works of literature and art produced at the same time or about similar themes or topics and how these may have influenced the text
- the ideas that were commonly believed at the time the text was written and how these are relevant to it.

> **context** the circumstances that form the setting for a piece of literature and can help readers to understand it

Activity 1

Complete the table below by filling in the right-hand column with comments about how each aspect of context might link to the text.

Facts about context	Link to the text
Golding started writing straight after the end of the Second World War.	Voting and how we pick leaders; battles between the boys; how 'normal behaviour' changes during war
Golding had been a teacher at a boys' school.	
The novel was published in 1954, when class was still a big issue.	
Golding fought in the Second World War in the Navy and was involved in attacking enemy targets.	

At the time the novel was published, people were anxious about the threat of nuclear war.	
Golding grew up at a time when R.M. Ballantyne's novel *Coral Island* was a popular read.	
At the time the story was written, women's career choices were limited and most people still thought that a woman's place was in the home.	
At the time Golding was writing, the British Empire (which included countries like South Africa, Canada, Australia, India and Nigeria) was beginning to break up, so Britain was losing some of its power.	

Upgrade

On separate paper, copy and complete the following spider diagram by researching facts to go with each heading. This will help you build your own knowledge of the context of *Lord of the Flies*. Remember to check the truth and reliability of your research by checking it in more than one source. Avoid relying on just one website.

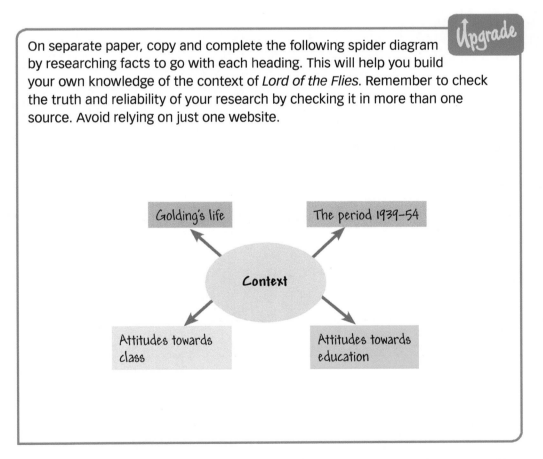

Remember, *knowing* about context is just the first step – to get marks you need to link context to Golding's choices in the novel. Let's practise this now.

Class

One aspect of the context of *Lord of the Flies* is how the novel explores ideas about **class**. This may seem an old-fashioned concept to modern readers, but at the time the novel was written and published the class system was still evident in society, with money and education both being factors that could affect people's perceptions of each other and access to different opportunities.

> **class** ordering of society where people are divided into sets based on perceived social or economic status

Activity 2

a) To delve into class and education in *Lord of the Flies*, scan through the first two chapters of the novel and identify who the speaker is for each quotation in the table below. Then complete the table by commenting on what each quotation suggests about the speaker's class background and education.

Quotation	Who said this?	Class/education
"I could swim when I was five. Daddy taught me." *(Chapter 1)*		
"Choir! Stand still!" *(Chapter 1)*		
"We're English; and the English are best at everything." *(Chapter 2)*		
"I was the only boy in our school what had asthma." *(Chapter 1)*		
"We'll have to have 'Hands up' like at school." *(Chapter 2)*		

b) At this point in Chapter 1 Golding does not bother to distinguish the speakers. Name all the potential speakers and comment on why you think Golding has not made it clear who is saying what.

> "Wacco."
>
> "Wizard."
>
> "Smashing." *(Chapter 1)*

As the novel goes on, class difference is not referred to as much as in the early chapters, perhaps because Golding tries to show how the experience of being on the island levels things out between the boys and erodes the differences between them.

Literary connections

Another important aspect of the context of the novel comes from its literary connections. In writing *Lord of the Flies*, Golding has very consciously drawn on a tradition of stories in which characters have adventures on islands.

Read the short extract below from Chapter 2. Ralph is reporting on the exploration of the island that he, Jack and Simon undertook. Notice how positive the boys are at this stage about the island. During the conversation, three other books about islands are mentioned: *Treasure Island*, *Swallows and Amazons* and *Coral Island*.

"But this is a good island. We – Jack, Simon and me – we climbed the mountain. It's wizard. There's food and drink, and –"

"Rocks –"

"Blue flowers –"

Piggy, partly recovered, pointed to the conch in Ralph's hands, and Jack and Simon fell silent. Ralph went on.

"While we're waiting we can have a good time on this island."

He gesticulated widely.

"It's like in a book."

At once there was a clamour.

"Treasure Island –"

"Swallows and Amazons –"

"Coral Island –"

Ralph waved the conch.

"This is our island. It's a good island. Until the grown-ups come to fetch us we'll have fun."

(Chapter 2)

Upgrade

Try to get hold of copies of the three other novels mentioned. You may not have time to read all of them but at least read the opening chapters and skim through to find scenes in which island life and the nature of the islands in each book is described. This will help you to make knowledgeable comparisons with *Lord of the Flies*.

Activity 3

Find out as much as you can about the novels referred to on page 19. Complete the table below to build your awareness of *Lord of the Flies*' literary context and how it compares to the other texts.

	Lord of the Flies	Treasure Island	Swallows and Amazons	Coral Island
Date written and author				
Name(s) and age(s) of main characters				
Heroes/villains – who they are and main actions				
Example description/ main features of the island				
Main events				
How the novel ends				

Developing your understanding of context

Showing a developed understanding of context in your writing about the novel means linking Golding's authorial choices to the context of his writing. The following activities will help you to do this.

Activity 4

Reread this extract from Chapter 12. Use the questions on page 22 as a guide as you annotate the extract and then answer the questions.

A naval officer stood on the sand, looking down at Ralph in wary astonishment. On the beach behind him was a cutter, her bows hauled up and held by two ratings. In the stern-sheets another rating held a sub-machine gun.

The ululation faltered and died away.

The officer looked at Ralph doubtfully for a moment, then took his hand away from the butt of the revolver.

"Hullo."

Squirming a little, conscious of his filthy appearance, Ralph answered shyly.

"Hullo."

The officer nodded, as if a question had been answered.

"Are there any adults – any grown-ups with you?"

Dumbly, Ralph shook his head. He turned a half-pace on the sand. A semicircle of little boys, their bodies streaked with coloured clay, sharp sticks in their hands, were standing on the beach making no noise at all.

"Fun and games," said the officer.

The fire reached the coco-nut palms by the beach and swallowed them noisily. A flame, seemingly detached, swung like an acrobat and licked up the palm heads on the platform. The sky was black.

The officer grinned cheerfully at Ralph.

"We saw your smoke. What have you been doing? Having a war or something?"

Ralph nodded.

> The officer inspected the little scarecrow in front of him. The kid needed a bath, a hair-cut, a nose-wipe and a good deal of ointment.
>
> "Nobody killed, I hope? Any dead bodies?"
>
> "Only two. And they've gone."
>
> The officer leaned down and looked closely at Ralph.
>
> "Two? Killed?"
>
> Ralph nodded again. Behind him, the whole island was shuddering with flame. The officer knew, as a rule, when people were telling the truth. He whistled softly.
>
> *(Chapter 12)*

a) With reference to the context of recent war, why do you think Golding introduces a naval officer at the end of the novel? Why has Golding referred to weapons?

----

b) In the context of Ralph's class and family background, explain the significance of his appearance in this passage.

----

c) How do the references to boys and typical boys' games highlight what has happened to the boys on the island?

All boys

Lord of the Flies is a story about British boys. It features no girls and no one from any other culture. This all-male Britishness is another important aspect of the novel's context, linked to the mid-20th century origins of the novel. At this time, women's career choices were limited and most people still thought that a woman's place was in the home. Britain was still in charge of an empire which included countries like South Africa, Canada, Australia, India and Nigeria. At the time of writing, the empire was beginning to break up, so Britain was losing some of its power.

Activity 5

Read this extract from an interview with William Golding to help you think about the all-male context of the novel. Annotate the extract using the questions on page 24 as a guide, then answer the questions, giving reasons for each answer.

"I was once a little boy - I have been a brother, a father, I am going to be a grandfather. I have never been a sister, or a mother, or a grandmother. That's one answer. Another answer is of course to say that if you – as it were – scaled down human beings, scaled down society, if you land with a group of little boys, they are more like a scaled-down version of society than a group of little girls would be. Don't ask me why, and this is a terrible thing to say because I'm going to be chased from hell to breakfast by all the women who talk about equality – this is nothing to do with equality at all. I think women are foolish to pretend they are equal to men, they are far superior and always have been. But one thing you can't do with them is take a bunch of them and boil them down, so to speak, into a set of little girls who would then become a kind of image of civilisation, of society. The other thing is – why aren't they little boys AND little girls? Well, if they'd been little boys and little girls, we being who we are, sex would have raised its lovely head, and I didn't want this to be about sex. Sex is too trivial a thing to get in with a story like this, which was about the problem of evil and the problem of how people are to live together in a society, not just as lovers or man and wife."

a) Golding implies that men can't write about women and women can't write about men – do you agree? Can you think of examples of books to back up or refute his view?

----

b) Do you think *Lord of the Flies* would have been more realistic if it had featured female characters? If a similar book were written now, would it have to include girls?

----

c) Do you agree with Golding that a group of girls would not represent an 'image of society'?

----

d) Golding says that he didn't include boys and girls in the story because then he would have had to write about sex, which, he argues, is 'trivial' compared to 'the problem of evil'. Do you agree?

Britishness

Activity 6

How important is the British context of the novel?

a) In bullet points and using short quotations from the text as evidence, on separate paper jot down the arguments you could make for each of the following statements about the novel's context:

- Golding is interested in ideas about Britishness.
- Golding wanted his characters to reflect pride in Britishness.
- Golding wanted the novel to show how a society could break down.

b) Annotate the extract from Chapter 5 below to show how it explores the context of Britishness, using the questions below and on page 26 for guidance. Then answer the questions.

> Ralph peered at the child in the twilight.
>
> "Now tell us. What's your name?"
>
> "Percival Wemys Madison, The Vicarage, Harcourt St. Anthony, Hants, telephone, telephone, tele –"
>
> As if this information was rooted far down in the springs of sorrow, the littlun wept. His face puckered, the tears leapt from his eyes, his mouth opened till they could see a square black hole. At first he was a silent effigy of sorrow; but then the lamentation rose out of him, loud and sustained as the conch.
>
> "Shut up, you! Shut up!"
>
> Percival Wemys Madison would not shut up. A spring had been tapped, far beyond the reach of authority or even physical intimidation. The crying went on, breath after breath, and seemed to sustain him upright as if he were nailed to it.
>
> "Shut up! Shut up!"
>
> For now the littluns were no longer silent. They were reminded of their personal sorrows; and perhaps felt themselves to share in a sorrow that was universal. They began to cry in sympathy, two of them almost as loud as Percival.
>
> *(Chapter 5)*

i. Someone has taught this child to recite his name and address. Who do you think it was and why? In what way could this now be described as ironic?

----

ii. Golding does not tell us who is telling Percival to "shut up"? Why not? And why is the phrase repeated, with exclamation marks?

----

iii. What aspects of British society might Golding be referring to when he mentions 'the reach of authority' and 'physical intimidation'?

----

iv. Why is it significant to Golding's exploration of Britishness that Percival's crying sets off the other littluns?

----

v. Compare this scene to what happens when Percival tries to recite his name in Chapter 12, by linking the scenes to the context of Britishness.

Progress check

Use the chart below to review the skills you have developed in this chapter.
For each column, start at the bottom box and work your way up towards the
highest level in the top box. Tick the box to show you have achieved that level.

I can sustain a critical response to *Lord of the Flies* and interpret the context convincingly ☐	I can show a perceptive understanding of how *Lord of the Flies* is shaped by its context ☐
I can develop a coherent response to *Lord of the Flies* and explain the context clearly ☐	I understand the context of *Lord of the Flies* and can make connections between the text and its context ☐
I can make some comments on the context in *Lord of the Flies* ☐	I am aware of the context in which *Lord of the Flies* was written ☐
Personal response	**Text and context**

Character overview

Knowing the characters of *Lord of the Flies* – their physical appearance, their traits and how they change – is an important part of knowing the whole text, as is understanding of their roles and functions and how Golding uses them.

Activity 1

Using your knowledge of the characters and rereading the text as you need to, complete the character profile cards below and on page 29, for each of these main characters.

Name: Ralph

First appears: ....
....
....
....

Last appears: ....
....
....
....

Object most closely linked with:
....
....
....

Functions as a symbol of:
....
....
....

Main actions: ....
....
....
....

Score out of 10 for:

- Bravery ___   • Loyalty ___
- Aggression ___ • Evil ___
- Pessimism ___   • How he changes ___

Name: Jack

First appears: ....
....
....
....

Last appears: ....
....
....
....

Object most closely linked with:
....
....
....

Functions as a symbol of:
....
....
....

Main actions: ....
....
....
....

Score out of 10 for:

- Bravery ___   • Loyalty ___
- Aggression ___ • Evil ___
- Pessimism ___   • How he changes ___

Name: Simon

First appears: ....
....
....
....

Last appears: ....
....
....
....

Object most closely linked with:
....
....
....

Functions as a symbol of:
....
....
....

Main actions: ....
....
....
....

Score out of 10 for:

- Bravery ___   • Loyalty ___
- Aggression ___ • Evil ___
- Pessimism ___   • How he changes ___

Name: Roger

First appears: ------------------

Last appears: ------------------

Object most closely linked with:

Functions as a symbol of:

Main actions: ------------------

Score out of 10 for:
- Bravery __
- Loyalty __
- Aggression __
- Evil __
- Pessimism __
- How he changes __

Name: Piggy

First appears: ------------------

Last appears: ------------------

Object most closely linked with:

Functions as a symbol of:

Main actions: ------------------

Score out of 10 for:
- Bravery __
- Loyalty __
- Aggression __
- Evil __
- Pessimism __
- How he changes __

Name: Samneric

First appears: ------------------

Last appears: ------------------

Object most closely linked with:

Functions as a symbol of:

Main actions: ------------------

Score out of 10 for:
- Bravery __
- Loyalty __
- Aggression __
- Evil __
- Pessimism __
- How they change __

Key quotation

The owner of the voice came backing out of the undergrowth so that twigs scratched on a greasy wind-breaker. The naked crooks of his knees were plump, caught and scratched by thorns. He bent down, removed the thorns carefully, and turned around. He was shorter than the fair boy and very fat. (*Chapter 1*)

Activity 2

Using the profile cards you have developed as a starting point, make a collection of three key quotations for each of the characters. Choose quotations from different parts of the text to make sure you have good knowledge of the development of characters.

Character	Key quotations
Ralph	
Jack	
Simon	
Roger	

Character	Key quotations
Piggy	
Samneric	

Upgrade

Comparing characters can lead to new insights and increase your understanding of them. Pick two characters that contrast in some way. For example, one might have stronger leadership qualities while the other is kinder. Use your character notes to answer the question that follows. Continue on separate paper if you need to.

Compare two characters, explaining with examples how they are different and how they change during the novel.

Leadership

The ability to lead is an aspect of character that is explored throughout *Lord of the Flies*. The post-war context of the novel – when memories of leaders such as Hitler and Churchill would have been fresh – makes this an idea that Golding is interested in; one important aspect of the novel is how he reflects on different styles and types of leader.

Activity 3

a) Use the following table to compare the leadership abilities of the boys. Write a note and/or quotation into each box to prove how each character shows each quality, using the first box in Piggy's column as a model. If you cannot find an example of a character demonstrating one of the qualities, write 'no evidence'. This should only happen two or three times across the table.

b) Complete the final row by evaluating, in your own words, each character's leadership ability based on the textual evidence.

	Ralph	Jack	Piggy	Simon
Intelligence			Knows what the conch is (Ch 1). "We could make a sundial" (Ch 4). Probably the cleverest boy on the island.	
Authority				
Power				
Reason				
Likeability				
Overall leadership ability				

Activity 4

Using your leadership comparison table (Activity 3) and your other knowledge of the boys, answer the following questions.

a) Apart from the qualities listed in the table, what other traits (such as strength, bossiness or bravery, for example) might be required for good leadership? Thinking about ALL the characters, who demonstrates these and when?

----

b) Does any single character possess every quality that is needed to be a good leader? What do you think Golding was suggesting by writing the book in this way?

Key quotation

The dark boy, Roger, stirred at last and spoke up.

"Let's have a vote."   *(Chapter 1)*

Characterization

Having a sense of how characters change, or do not change, will help you to show a deeper understanding of the novel. Golding uses **characterization** as a way to present different aspects of the ideas he is exploring.

characterization
the ways that fictional characters are created or constructed

Activity 5

Complete the following tables for Jack, Simon, Piggy and Ralph to consider how characters develop.

Jack

	Two sentences in your own words	Two short quotations to back up your points	Two sentences about how Jack is used to present ideas. You can use the prompt phrases suggested, or similar ones of your own
At the beginning of the novel, Jack is...			This shows that... What ideas does Jack stand for at the beginning of the book?
In the middle chapters, Jack... Look at Chapters 3, 5 and 8.			Golding suggests that... The scene highlights...
By the end of the novel, Jack...			Jack is a symbol of... Golding seems to be saying that...

Simon

	Two sentences in your own words	Two short quotations to back up your points	Two sentences about how Simon is used to present ideas. You can use the prompt phrases suggested, or similar ones of your own
At the beginning of the novel, Simon is... Note that the first appearance of Simon is when he faints in Chapter 1, and he then is chosen as the third boy in Ralph and Jack's scouting party.			Golding uses Simon to...
In the middle chapters, Simon...			Simon's communication with the Lord of the Flies represents...
By the end of the novel, Simon...			Simon's death shows that... Simon is dead by the time rescue arrives. How does this appear to the naval officer?

As you probably will not be allowed to take the text into the exam, learning a few short quotations by heart, like the ones you have used here, is also a good idea.

Piggy

	Two sentences in your own words	Two short quotations to back up your points	Two sentences about how Piggy is used to present ideas. You can use the prompt phrases suggested, or similar ones of your own
At the beginning of the novel, Piggy is... Consider Piggy's speech and appearance.			Golding's initial presentation of Piggy shows that...
In the middle chapters, Piggy...			Golding uses Piggy to...
By the end of the novel, Piggy...			Overall, Piggy is important because... Consider the values that Piggy symbolizes and why he is killed.

Ralph

	Two sentences in your own words	Two short quotations to back up your points	Two sentences about how Ralph is being used to present ideas. You can use the prompt phrases suggested, or similar ones of your own
At the beginning of the novel, Ralph is...			From the very beginning, Ralph represents...
In the middle chapters, Ralph... Compare some of the different relationships and emotions Ralph experiences.			Golding uses Ralph to stand for...
By the end of the novel, Ralph...			The final image of Ralph is important because... Compare the first and last times we see Ralph in the novel.

Developing your understanding of characters

Knowing characters and being able to describe and comment on their development is a good start. However, applying your knowledge of character, and writing insightfully about how Golding uses characters to tell different aspects of the story, are key skills for the higher grades. In the sample answer in Activity 7 the student is struggling to do it – the student knows the characters, but does not apply their knowledge to develop their ideas. The question they are trying to answer is:

> How is Piggy perceived by others during the novel, and what does this suggest about Golding's ideas about mankind?

Activity 6

Read the student's answer and use the questions below it to suggest improvements.

At the start, Piggy is seen as a fat boy who is totally uncomfortable on the island. He has "ass-mar". Even when he is struggling for breath "his mouth gaping, blue shadows creeping round his lips", the other boys ignore him. This suggests that what he stands for isn't very important to the boys. The other boys seem to judge him. He is intelligent but this doesn't count for much. For example, even though Piggy is the one who knows what the conch is, he gets told to "shut up" when he wants to use it. This represents Golding's ideas about democracy.

Piggy is perceived differently by the older boys and the littluns. Jack is probably the most dismissive towards Piggy. All the older ones know his glasses are important but they don't value him in other ways. For example, Ralph makes fun of him when he suggesting they "make a sundial". With the littluns, he is often in charge, which makes him seem most like an adult, and he calls the others "a pack of kids".

Just before Piggy's death, Golding uses him to stand up for basic values, like "law and rescue" and being "sensible". The killing of Piggy is a comment on the death of reason and straight thinking on the island.

a) Ralph is the first boy we see react to Piggy – what is his attitude to Piggy's 'ass-mar'? Why do you think Golding hasn't made Ralph more sympathetic?

----

b) What does Piggy stand for? Give two examples, using short quotes to back up your ideas.

----

c) Give an example of how the others judge him and say why Golding has him treated in this way.

----

d) Be specific: as Piggy is of a lower class than the other boys, what is Golding saying about democracy when no one listens to him even when he's holding the conch?

----

e) Give an example of this.

----

f) Develop this. If Piggy stands for adult values, why do you think the others do not listen to him?

Upgrade

Notice that the student who attempted this answer about Piggy is doing well at embedding quotations within their response. By structuring their own sentences to incorporate these short phrases from the text, they show a very close awareness of the text but without having to memorize and write out long quotations.

Ralph

As the story of *Lord of the Flies* begins and ends with Ralph and much of the action revolves around him, we can make a good case that he is the main character. Other clues to this are that his point of view is used to tell the story more than that of any of the other characters. We even see him dreaming about and remembering his past.

Activity 7

Reread the quotations below. Annotate them using the questions about Ralph on page 41 as a guide, then answer the questions.

> Ralph was dreaming. He had fallen asleep after what seemed hours of tossing and turning noisily among the dry leaves. Even the sounds of nightmare from the other shelters no longer reached him, for he was back to where he came from, feeding the ponies with sugar over the garden wall. Then someone was shaking his arm, telling him that it was time for tea. (*Chapter 6*)

> Once, following his father from Chatham to Devonport, they had lived in a cottage on the edge of the moors. In the succession of houses that Ralph had known, this one stood out with particular clarity because after that house he had been sent away to school. Mummy had still been with them and Daddy had come home every day. Wild ponies came to the stone wall at the bottom of the garden, and it had snowed. ...
>
> When you went to bed there was a bowl of cornflakes with sugar and cream. And the books – they stood on the shelf by the bed, leaning together with always two or three laid flat on top because he had not bothered to put them back properly. They were dog-eared and scratched. There was the bright, shining one about Topsy and Mopsy that he never read because it was about two girls; there was the one about the Magician which you read with a kind of tied-down terror, skipping page twenty-seven with the awful picture of the spider; there was a book about people who had dug things up, Egyptian things; there was *the Boy's Book of Trains, The Boy's Book of Ships*. Vividly they came before him; he could have reached up and touched them, could feel the weight and slow slide with which the *Mammoth Book for Boys* would come out and slither down. ... Everything was all right; everything was good-humoured and friendly. (*Chapter 7*)

> Supposing they could be transported home by jet, then before morning they would land at that big airfield in Wiltshire. They would go by car; no, for things to be perfect they would go by train; all the way down to Devon and take that cottage again. Then at the foot of the garden the wild ponies would come and look over the wall. ...
>
> Ralph turned restlessly in the leaves. Dartmoor was wild and so were the ponies. But the attraction of wildness had gone.
>
> His mind skated to a consideration of a tamed town where savagery could not set foot. What could be safer than the bus centre with its lamps and wheels? (Chapter 10)

a) Why do you think Ralph is dreaming of his past and his roots at each of these points?

----

b) What images are used and what do they suggest about Ralph's childhood?

----

c) How important are Ralph's parents at the time of each memory?

----

d) How do the objects that Ralph daydreams of suggest the things he misses?

The quotations about Ralph's dreams and memories come from different places in the novel. The first is from just after the dead parachutist is mistaken for the beast by Sam and Eric. The second daydream takes place while Jack hunts. The third quotation is from the moment just before Ralph's camp is ambushed by Jack's gang and Piggy's glasses are stolen.

Activity 8

a) In your own words, summarize the content of Ralph's dreams.

----

b) Why do you think Golding shows Ralph dreaming of these things at these moments?

Critical understanding

Analysing character means being able to dwell on detail and speculate on the author's choice of vocabulary and other characterization choices. Here is an extract from a student's work in which character analysis is being done very well. The student is answering the question: 'How does Golding use the character of Roger to explore the idea of power?'

From Roger's first appearance as 'a slight, furtive boy whom no one knew', Golding positions him as an outsider. He isn't part of Jack's choir, even though he later aligns himself with the hunters, and the author hints at his later actions by describing him as having 'an inner intensity'. However, this characterization doesn't mean he isn't powerful. In fact, he makes one of the most important contributions to democracy on the island, by suggesting a vote. Interestingly, immediately after this, Jack, Piggy and Ralph are all mentioned in the paragraph that follows, reminding the reader of their three-way struggle for power, but Roger reverts to his usual silence.

In Chapter 4, a key scene involving Roger shows his developing importance and foreshadows later events. As he throws stones at Henry, one of the younger children, Golding emphasizes his meanness. Roger waits until he and the other child are alone, and then throws stones at him. Golding suggests that Roger is copying or being influenced by the behaviour of the wild island, as this follows straight on from the 'cluster of nuts... loosed from their stems' by a breeze landing all around him. But, at this stage, Roger has not fully let go of 'the taboo of the old life' and his power is limited: Henry walks away unhurt.

Activity 9

a) Review the extract from the student essay above against the success criteria for effective character analysis below. Place a tick or a cross next to each criterion.

	Student's extract	My extract
Short quotations embedded		
Comments on Golding's use of the character		
Links to Golding's ideas		
Focus on 'power' as required by the question		
Knowledge of the whole text shown by linking a range of scenes		
Events mentioned only briefly with much more focus on what they mean		

b) Write your own paragraph of character analysis to continue the response to the question 'How does Golding use the character of Roger to explore the idea of power?' Continue on separate paper if you need to. Your section of the essay should focus on the second half of the book. For example, you could refer to:

- the scene when Roger kills Piggy (Chapter 8)
- Samneric's fear of Roger's sharpened stick (Chapter 12)
- Roger's part in the hunting of Ralph (Chapter 13).

----

c) Assess your work by checking it against the same success criteria (see Activity 10a).

Progress check

Use the chart below to review the skills you have developed in this chapter. For each column, start at the bottom box and work your way up towards the highest level in the top box. Tick the box to show you have achieved that level.

Personal response	Textual references
I can sustain a critical response to *Lord of the Flies* and interpret the characters convincingly ☐	I can use well-integrated textual references from *Lord of the Flies* to support my interpretation ☐
I can develop a coherent response to *Lord of the Flies* and explain the characters clearly ☐	I can use quotations and other textual references from *Lord of the Flies* to support my explanation ☐
I can make some comments on the characters in *Lord of the Flies* ☐	I can make references to some details from *Lord of the Flies* ☐

Literal understanding

Lord of the Flies is a richly textured novel layered with meanings. This means that almost every sentence is a gift to a student who must comment on and analyse the language. The key to doing this well is to notice detail and be prepared to see beyond literal meanings to subtler, concealed meanings.

Activity 1

a) Read the following quotations and then match them to their literal meanings on page 45.

1

> Roger led the way straight through the castles, kicking them over, burying the flowers, scattering the chosen stones.
> *(Chapter 4)*

2

> Jack himself shrank at this cry [of a bird] with a hiss of indrawn breath; and for a minute became less a hunter than a furtive thing, ape-like among the tangle of trees.
> *(Chapter 3)*

3

> This wind pressed his grey shirt against his chest so that he noticed – in this new mood of comprehension – how the folds were stiff like cardboard, and unpleasant...
> *(Chapter 5)*

4

> The water rose further and dressed Simon's coarse hair with brightness. The line of his cheek silvered and the turn of his shoulder became sculptured marble.
> *(Chapter 9)*

Literal meaning

This character is not always brave when he is hunting.   [-------]

The body is swept into the water.   [-------]

The island is making this character physically uncomfortable.   [-------]

This character is mean to the younger children.   [-------]

b) Highlight a word or phrase in each quotation that helps you understand the literal meanings.

c) Now read the quotations again and match them to their subtle meanings.

Subtle meaning

[-------]   The character's journey from civilization to wildness is shown in the way he adopts animal noises and is described as an animal.

[-------]   Representing pointless destruction, this behaviour foreshadows other violence like the killing of Piggy.

[-------]   Golding shows the power of the island environment and the character's reaction to it.

[-------]   The language suggests the character has saintly qualities or resembles a heavenly statue.

d) Annotate each quotation to explain how Golding conveys the subtle meaning.

Language features

To comment effectively on language, you need an understanding of the tools an author uses to create different effects. Here is an example paragraph from Chapter 4, annotated to highlight the language features to look out for in any section of *Lord of the Flies*.

imagery visually descriptive or figurative language, especially simile and metaphor

Layers of meaning – yes, Piggy is alone for the moment, but he is also an outsider from the beginning of the novel.

Piggy stood behind him, islanded in a sea of meaningless colour, while Ralph knelt and focused the glossy spot. Instantly the fire was alight Piggy held out his hand and grabbed the glasses back. Before these fantastically attractive flowers of violet and red and yellow, unkindness melted away. They became a circle of boys round a camp fire and even Piggy and Ralph were half-drawn in. Soon some of the boys were rushing down the slope for more wood while Jack hacked the pig. They tried holding the whole carcass on a stake over the fire, but the stake burnt more quickly than the pig roasted. In the end they skewered bits of meat on branches and held them in the flames; and even then almost as much boy was roasted as meat.

Ralph dribbled. He meant to refuse meat but his past diet of fruit and nuts, with an odd crab or fish, gave him too little resistance. He accepted a piece of half-raw meat and gnawed it like a wolf.

Piggy spoke, also dribbling.

"Aren't I having none?"

Adjectives that help to make the environment seem positive or negative – here the fire is described in warm and inviting terms because the boys are eating their first killed pig, but later fire becomes hugely threatening.

Foreshadowing/echoing – watch out for any moments that foreshadow or echo others, like this reference to Jack's violence that shows him as being in charge, which should make you think about later events when he becomes chief.

Verbs that suggest savagery – compare Ralph's dribbling here to the way he would have been expected to eat in civilized society.

Animalistic **imagery** – there are many times in the novel where Golding compares the boys to animals.

Speech and dialect – Golding creates different voices for the characters to remind us of their class and background.

Activity 2

Use the annotations from the example on page 46 to help you analyse this new text extract from Chapter 9. The arrows have been supplied to help you see where to focus.

> The circle became a horseshoe. A thing was crawling out of the forest. It came darkly, uncertainly. The shrill screaming that rose before the beast was like a pain. The beast stumbled into the horseshoe.
>
> *"Kill the beast! Cut his throat! Spill his blood!"*
>
> The blue-white scar was constant, the noise unendurable. Simon was crying out something about a dead man on a hill.
>
> *"Kill the beast! Cut his throat! Spill his blood! Do him in!"*
>
> The sticks fell and the mouth of the new circle crunched and screamed. The beast was on its knees in the centre, its arms folded over its face. It was crying out against the abominable noise something about a body on the hill. The beast struggled forward, broke the ring and fell over the steep edge of the rock to the sand by the water. At once the crowd surged after it, poured down the rock, leapt on to the beast, screamed, struck, bit, tore. There were no words, and no movements but the tearing of teeth and claws.

To access higher grades, develop your annotations by adding explanations of the effect of the language choices Golding has made.

Developing your understanding of language

Interpreting layers of meaning as you did in Activity 1 is a good starting point for developing your understanding of language. However, for higher grades you need to comment in detail on Golding's language choices.

Activity 3

Here are the quotations from Activity 1 again. This time, the original comments on the subtler meaning need to be developed to include more detailed analysis of language.

a) An example has been completed for you. Using the third column, develop all of the original comments in a similar way.

Quotations	Original comment	Developed comment
'Jack himself shrank at this cry [of a bird] with a hiss of indrawn breath; and for a minute became less a hunter than a furtive thing, ape-like among the tangle of trees.' *(Chapter 3)*	The character's journey from civilization to wildness is shown in the way he adopts animal noises and is described as an animal.	
'Roger led the way straight through the castles, kicking them over, burying the flowers, scattering the chosen stones.' *(Chapter 4)*	Representing pointless destruction, this behaviour foreshadows other violence like the killing of Piggy.	
'The wind pressed his grey shirt against his chest so that he noticed – in this new mood of comprehension – how the folds were stiff like cardboard, and unpleasant...' *(Chapter 5)*	Golding shows the power of the island environment and the character's reaction to it.	His 'new mood of comprehension', emphasized by the dashes in the sentence, suggests that his view of the 'good island' (Chapter 2) is changing as his shirt, a symbol of school and civilization, becomes uncomfortable.
'The water rose further and dressed Simon's coarse hair with brightness. The line of his cheek silvered and the turn of his shoulder became sculptured marble.' *(Chapter 9)*	The language suggests the character has saintly qualities or resembles a heavenly statue.	

b) For each quotation in the table, find another example of a time in the novel when Golding uses a similar language technique, and comment on the effect.

Quotations	Another example of this technique	Effect of Golding's language at this point in the novel
'Jack himself shrank at this cry [of a bird] with a hiss of indrawn breath; and for a minute became less a hunter than a furtive thing, ape-like among the tangle of trees.' *(Chapter 3)*		
'Roger led the way straight through the castles, kicking them over, burying the flowers, scattering the chosen stones.' *(Chapter 4)*		
'The wind pressed his grey shirt against his chest so that he noticed – in this new mood of comprehension – how the folds were stiff like cardboard, and unpleasant...' *(Chapter 5)*		
'The water rose further and dressed Simon's coarse hair with brightness. The line of his cheek silvered and the turn of his shoulder became sculptured marble.' *(Chapter 9)*		

Personification

Personification is a technique used regularly by Golding. It helps to create atmosphere and a vivid visual picture in the reader's head. Golding uses personification to:

- draw parallels between the wildness of nature and the growing wildness of the boys
- make the natural environment seem like an enemy
- show the impact the boys have on nature.

> **personification** a type of metaphor where human qualities are given to objects or ideas

 Activity 4

a) Read the following quotations, which all include examples of personification. In each quotation, highlight the words chosen by Golding that give the object human qualities.

b) Find each quotation in your copy of the text and reread the relevant section of the novel. Make notes on what you think the chosen words suggest about the natural environment. Be precise. For example:

The words 'leapt nimbly' give the impression that the fire is light-footed and fast-moving but are not particularly menacing.

i.
> The flames, as though they were a kind of wild life, crept as a jaguar creeps on its belly towards a line of birch-like saplings that fledged an outcrop of the pink rock. They flapped at the first of the trees, and the branches grew a brief foliage of fire. The heart of flame leapt nimbly across the gap between the trees… *(Chapter 2)*

----

ii.
> A flurry of wind made the palms talk and the noise seemed very loud now that darkness and silence made it so noticeable. Two grey trunks rubbed each other with an evil squeaking that no one had noticed by day. *(Chapter 5)*

---

iii.

> After a while these flies found Simon. Gorged, they alighted by his runnels of sweat and drank. They tickled under his nostrils and played leap-frog on his thighs. *(Chapter 8)*

---

iv.

> … and there was the fathom-wide grin of the skull, no longer ridiculing a deep blue patch of sky but jeering up into a blanket of smoke…. He could see the sun-splashed ground over an area of perhaps fifty yards from where he lay: and as he watched, the sunlight in every patch blinked at him. *(Chapter 12)*

Pathetic fallacy

The island, nature and the weather are important throughout the story. To help show this, Golding uses another well-established technique, called **pathetic fallacy**, exploiting the natural environment to enhance the atmosphere at different points.

> **pathetic fallacy** a literary technique that gives human qualities or emotions to inanimate objects of nature; for example, when weather is used to reflect a particular mood

Activity 5

Find events a, b and c in the text, and check the natural conditions Golding describes for each. Then insert them in the right place in the table below. Finally, add a commentary in the third column to show why Golding's choice of weather at each moment is significant.

a) The expedition to Castle Rock to find the beast, the first time the boys go there.

b) Simon's murder.

c) The first gathering on the beach, including the appearance of the choir.

Natural conditions	Event	Why is the choice of natural conditions significant at this moment?
Hot sunshine causing mirages (Chapter 1)		
The Pacific Ocean swelling and heaving (Chapter 6)		
Thunderstorm with lightning (Chapter 9)		

Juxtaposition

Another linguistic trick to watch out for when you are reading *Lord of the Flies* is the use of contrasts and **juxtaposition**.

Consider the following example from Chapter 4.

> **juxtaposition** placing two opposite ideas or meanings near or next to each other to draw attention to the similarities or contrasts between them

Short simple sentence to introduce the face-off.

Positive and negative adjectives contrasted.

> The two boys faced each other. There was the brilliant world of hunting, tactics, fierce exhilaration, skill; and there was the world of longing and baffled common-sense.

Repetition of phrase to introduce the two lists emphasizes the contrast.

A list of ideas that represent Jack.

Activity 6

Annotate the following examples of juxtaposition from Chapters 1 and 5 using the example above as a guide.

> The fat boy waited to be asked his name in turn but this proffer of acquaintance was not made; the fair boy called Ralph smiled vaguely, stood up, and began to make his way once more towards the lagoon. *(Chapter 1)*

> "Grown-ups know things," said Piggy. "They ain't afraid of the dark. They'd meet and have tea and discuss. Then things 'ud be all right –"
>
> "They wouldn't set fire to the island. Or lose – "
>
> "They'd build a ship –" *(Chapter 5)*

Narrative voice

The **narrative voice** of the novel is another interesting aspect of language. Golding uses a range of points of view to tell the story. Most of the time, he uses an **omniscient, third-person narrator**, telling the story from an all-knowing perspective. This means he can present the views and thoughts of a range of characters. This makes us feel very close to a character. Usually, the character whose **internal monologue** we hear is Ralph, but we also dip into other characters' thoughts and feelings.

> **internal monologue** when the reader feels as though they are inside a character's head because their thoughts are presented directly (without 'he said' or 'he thought')
>
> **narrative voice** the voice used to tell the story
>
> **omniscient narrator** a narrator who knows everything about the characters, including inner thoughts and feelings
>
> **third person** from the point of view of a character using the pronouns `he' or `she' (as opposed to first person, which uses the pronoun 'I')

Activity 7

Using the key term definitions about narrative voice and the completed example as a model, identify the narrative mode at each of the following points. Make sure you consider the reasons for Golding's chosen approach and comment on the effect created.

> This toy of voting was almost as pleasing as the conch. Jack started to protest but the clamour changed from the general wish for a chief to an election by acclaim of Ralph himself. *(Chapter 1)*

Here we see the third-person omniscient narrator observing the group, telling the reader about a range of characters. As this scene is all about democratic rule, when everyone has a say, it's interesting that Golding chooses a type of narration that gives an equal and all-round view of the boys. It means that the narrative style seems to match what it happening in the text.

a)

> In his other life Maurice had received chastisement for filling a younger eye with sand. Now, though there was no parent to let fall a heavy hand, Maurice still felt the unease of wrong-doing. At the back of his mind formed the uncertain outlines of an excuse. *(Chapter 4)*

b)

A sliver of moon rose over the horizon, hardly large enough to make a path of light even when it sat right down on the water; but there were other lights in the sky, that moved fast, winked, or went out, though not even a faint popping came down from the battle fought at ten miles' height. But a sign came down from the world of grown-ups, though at the time there was no child awake to read it. *(Chapter 6)*

c)

Simon… opened his eyes quickly and there was the head grinning amusedly in the strange daylight, ignoring the flies, the spilled guts, even ignoring the indignity of being spiked on a stick.

He looked away, licking his dry lips.

A gift for the beast. Might not the beast come for it? The head, he thought, appeared to agree with him. *(Chapter 8)*

d)

When Roger came to the neck of land that joined the Castle Rock to the mainland he was not surprised to be challenged. He had reckoned, during the terrible night, on finding at least some of the tribe holding out against the horrors of the island in the safest place. *(Chapter 10)*

e)

What was to be done then? The tree? Burst the line like a boar? Either way the choice was terrible.

A single cry quickened his heart-beat and, leaping up, he dashed away towards the ocean side and the thick jungle till he was hung up among creepers; he stayed there for a moment with his calves quivering. If only one could have pax, a long pause, a time to think! *(Chapter 12)*

Analysing language

To write successfully about language your answers need to go beyond naming linguistic features. You need to be able to analyse and interpret the effect of Golding's language choices in a coherent way. Notice the way this student is beginning to do this. This answer is in response to the question 'How does Golding use language in the opening chapter to introduce the ideas he goes on to explore?'

Specific language techniques mentioned.

Too many sentences beginning with 'this' make it clunky for the reader.

Some different connecting phrases used to make the text cohere and flow.

Comments on effect of Golding's use of language.

Some references to later parts of the book – do more of this.

From the very beginning, Golding uses language to contrast Ralph 'the fair boy' and Piggy 'the fat boy'. For a start, they speak differently, as Piggy has a colloquial voice revealing his lower-class background. They also have different physical features. Ralph is athletic – he jumps, swims and stands on his head. This is juxtaposed with Piggy's 'thick spectacles' and 'plump' knees. The effect of this is to make the reader compare the two boys. This becomes an important idea in the book because Ralph is chosen as leader but Piggy might be a better leader if he could win the boys' respect. Another linguistic feature that Golding uses is the way he describes the positive and negative aspects of the island. For example, the 'green shade', the coral reef and 'the incredible pool' make it sound like an idyllic place. However, Golding also creates sinister hints that life on the island may not always be so pleasant later on, such as the whispering palm-fronds and the 'decaying coco-nuts'.

Short embedded quotations.

Activity 8

Write a further paragraph to follow on from this student's work. Include:

- a further example of contrasting language and how it links to later developments in the novel
- an example of how Golding uses animal imagery and how it foreshadows ideas that come later
- an example of personification, its effect and how it relates to a later part of the novel.

- -

- -

- -

- -

- -

- -

Activity 9

Review the strengths and weaknesses of the student writing on page 56 and then assess
your own work by looking for similar features. Annotate your own writing to highlight
similar strengths and give advice to yourself on how you could do better next time.

Progress check

Use the chart below to review the skills you have developed in this chapter.
For each column, start at the bottom box and work your way up towards the
highest level in the top box. Tick the box to show you have achieved that level.

Textual references	Language, structure, form
I can use well-integrated textual references from *Lord of the Flies* to support my interpretation	I can analyse the effects of Golding's use of language, structure and form in *Lord of the Flies*, using subject terms judiciously
I can use quotations and other textual references from *Lord of the Flies* to support my explanation	I can explain how Golding uses language, structure and form to create effects in *Lord of the Flies*, using relevant subject terms
I can make references to some details from *Lord of the Flies*	I can identify some of Golding's methods in *Lord of the Flies* and use some subject terms

Textual references

Language, structure, form

Key ideas

Lord of the Flies is famous for its exploration of **themes** such as power and civilization, but Golding also considers other ideas in the novel and it is important to have a good grasp of them all.

> **theme** an idea that recurs in a work of literature

Activity 1

Consider the following spider diagram of some of the themes of the novel and identify a relevant moment from the text for each one. Write a short note about the moment you have chosen, using the completed example as a guide.

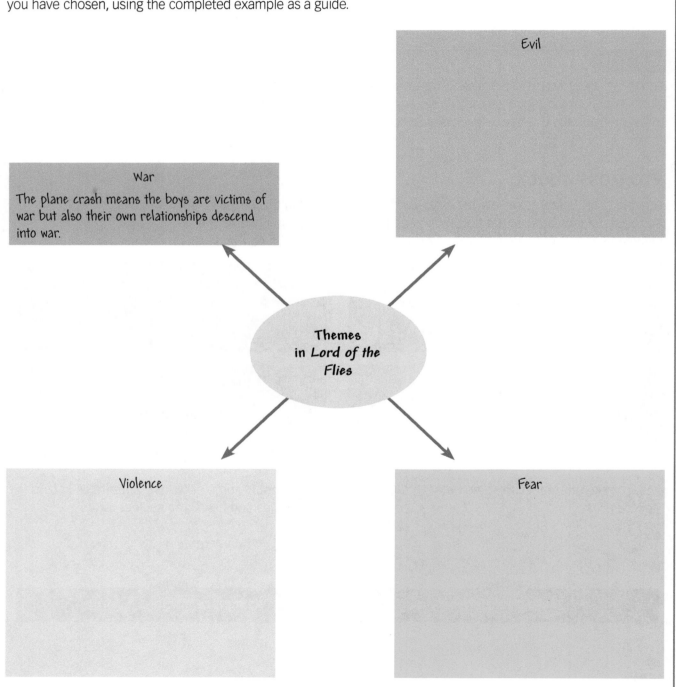

Evil

War
The plane crash means the boys are victims of war but also their own relationships descend into war.

Themes in *Lord of the Flies*

Violence

Fear

Activity 2

As you may have noticed, all the themes mentioned so far are rather negative ideas. Do you think the novel presents a completely negative view of the world, or does Golding have anything positive to say?

Creating a bank of quotations to help you explore the main themes in the text is a good idea. And re-reading the text, as required in the next activity, will help to make sure you know it really well and give you a great advantage when you have to write about it.

Activity 3

For each theme in the table on page 60 complete the following.

a) Add a relevant quotation from this selection to the second column.

'…there was a stillness about Ralph as he sat that marked him out: there was his size, and attractive appearance; and most obscurely, yet most powerfully, there was the conch.' *(Chapter 1)*

'Jack planned his new face. He made one cheek and one eye-socket white, then rubbed red over the other half of his face and slashed a black bar of charcoal across from right ear to left jaw.' *(Chapter 4)*

'…Piggy was an outsider, not only by accent, which did not matter, but by fat, and ass-mar, and specs, and a certain disinclination for manual labour.' *(Chapter 4)*

'This meeting must not be fun, but business.' *(Chapter 5)*

'Simon found he was looking into a vast mouth. There was blackness within, a blackness that spread.' *(Chapter 8)*

'The Chief led them, trotting steadily, exulting in his achievement. He was a chief now in truth; and he made stabbing motions with his spear.' *(Chapter 10)*

"Which is better – to have rules and agree, or to hunt and kill?" *(Chapter 11)*

b) Skim through and reread the text to find your own quotation to go with each idea and enter it in the third column.

Theme	Quotation from list provided	Own choice of relevant quotation
Loss of innocence		
Civilization		
Leadership		
Innate evil of humanity		
Power		
Class		
Identity		

Upgrade

Remember that embedding short quotations in your own writing about the text is a good way to save time (you do not want to be remembering or writing out massive sections of Golding's writing). Use a highlighter to identify a short phrase that could be embedded in your own writing from each of the quotations you've inserted in the table for Activity 3.

Linking themes

You have probably noticed that many of the ideas in *Lord of the Flies* are intertwined. For example, you can start off looking at the theme of leadership, which might lead you to ideas about power and then to the notion of violence. We could show this in a flow diagram:

> **Leadership** is an important idea in the novel. One of the first conflicts is between Ralph and Jack, when Ralph's control of the conch gives him the balance of…

⬇

> **Power**, however, power shifts away from Ralph later. Jack uses his hunters to get meat and challenges the importance of the fire. He also leads the boys into disordered 'noise and excitement, scramblings, screams and laughter', which descends eventually into…

⬇

> **Violence**, which leads, for example, to the deaths of Simon and Piggy.

Activity 4

Use the templates provided to create your own flow diagrams to show how ideas link together. You can insert your own choice of theme trios, or use these suggested ideas:

Civilization ⟶ Evil nature of mankind ⟶ Fear

Loss of innocence ⟶ Violence ⟶ War

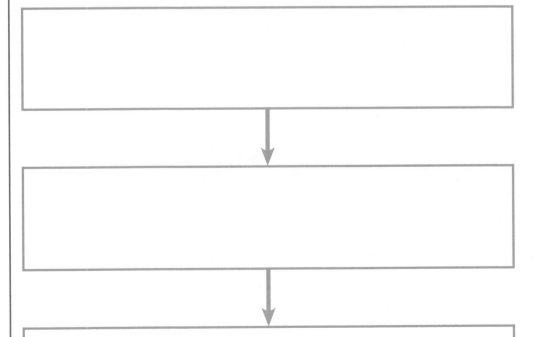

Symbols

Remember that themes are ideas that crop up again and again in a text. They are usually introduced in the early pages, and then referred to and developed as the novel goes on. But they may not always be obvious – Golding uses **symbols** to present recurring ideas. This means you need to be aware of the ideas represented by each symbol.

symbol a thing that represents or stands for something else

> **Key quotation**
>
> "We saw your smoke. What have you been doing? Having a war or something?" *(Chapter 12)*

Activity 5

Match each symbol listed on the left with the idea it stands for on the right.

The conch	Civilization
The scar	The adult world
Piggy's glasses	Rules and order
The island	The world
The pig's head (Lord of the Flies)	Humanity's innate evil
The dead pilot (parachutist)	Intelligence
School uniforms	Humanity's negative impact on the world

Upgrade

Which one of the symbols listed above do you consider to be most important and why?

Actions

As well as symbols, Golding also uses actions to explore ideas. As the story moves on, you will notice that plot events start to connect with symbols and characters to represent important themes. For example, the election of Ralph and his use of the conch in Chapter 1 can be said to introduce ideas about leadership, while the fire, started by Piggy's glasses and which then explodes out of control in Chapter 2, begins an exploration of the theme of disorder triumphing over intelligence.

Activity 6

a) Practise matching plot to theme by adding the following themes into the second column of the table below, so that they match up. Take care: some plot events are relevant to more than one theme.

Fear

Civilization

Power

Leadership

Humanity's innate evil

Intelligence

Loss of innocence

b) In the third column, write a short quotation relevant to each theme and event.

Plot events	Relevant theme(s)	Linked quotation
The dead parachutist is mistaken for a beast		
Jack discards his clothing		

Jack challenges Ralph's authority		
Piggy's glasses get broken		
Percival fails to recite his address		
Roger kills Piggy		

The author's values and attitudes

One of the main features of the novel's context is the author's intention when he wrote it. Many critics would argue that, on the one hand, Golding set out to write an adventure story but on the other, the book functions as an **allegory** that could be read as a statement about the nature of humanity and as a lesson about our times. Allegories work by using characters, events and objects to stand in for ideas that the author wants to explore.

allegory a story with a hidden meaning in which characters, events and objects have a symbolic function

Activity 7

Here is a list of characters, objects and events, all of which can be read as allegorical symbols. Complete the table to show what idea(s) each stands for. Two have been suggested to get you started.

Allegorical symbol	What does it stand for?
Adults	
Jack	
Piggy	
Piggy's glasses	
Ralph	
Simon	Goodness/Christ
The beast	
The conch	
The dead parachutist	
The fire	
The island at the beginning of the novel	The Garden of Eden before the arrival of the boys/the world before humanity has ruined it
The littluns	
The Lord of the Flies	
The scar	

Tracking themes

Tracking themes as they develop chapter by chapter should be an important element of your revision of the text because it will help you to demonstrate that you understand that the ideas are not static or simplistic. For example, you want to be able to move away from a simple statement like, 'Golding explores the idea of democracy in the novel' to being able to make a more thoughtful comment such as, 'Golding presents democracy as a fragile concept and shows how easily it is destroyed.'

Here is an activity to help you with this.

Activity 8

For four themes of your own choice, find references in at least four different chapters. In the boxes, insert the relevant chapter numbers (ensuring that you do this in chronological order) and a brief note about how that idea or theme is developed in the relevant chapter. The top table can be used as a guide – try to embed a relevant quotation in your commentary if you can.

	Chapter reference 1	Chapter reference 2
Democracy	Chapter 1 – Ralph and Piggy find the conch, a symbol of democracy. Piggy knows what it is but Ralph wields it first, showing his leadership skills – Golding aligns both boys with democratic ideas immediately.	Chapter 5 – Ralph observes that the conch is changing – 'exposure to the air had bleached the yellow and pink to near-white, and transparency'. This suggests the fragility of democracy, and we see the boys' ability to maintain fair rule begin to break down in this chapter.
	Chapter reference 3	**Chapter reference 4**
	Chapter 8 – Jack calls a meeting and later storms off crying. His claim to power is not established democratically. Ralph's ability to lead is declining – the boys are not listening to each other, with the dialogue showing many interruptions. But some of the boys still hold the conch in 'affectionate respect'.	Chapter 11 – Piggy is killed, and simultaneously, 'the conch exploded into a thousand white fragments and ceased to exist'. Jack has established a new power base at Castle Rock and the destruction of democracy is complete.

Chapter reference 1	Chapter reference 2
Chapter reference 3	**Chapter reference 4**

Chapter reference 1	Chapter reference 2
Chapter reference 3	Chapter reference 4

Chapter reference 1	Chapter reference 2
Chapter reference 3	Chapter reference 4

Chapter reference 1	Chapter reference 2
Chapter reference 3	Chapter reference 4

Interpreting ideas

Once you know how to read for a theme like this, in a way that tracks the development of ideas, you will be able to write very effectively and analytically about Golding's ideas. For example, here is the beginning of a student's answer to the question 'How does Golding present the boys' experience of democracy?'

You will be able to see from the teacher's comments what the strengths are of this piece of writing.

Good – a brief reference to the plot without retelling the story.

Relevant quotations embedded.

Effective use of key words of question used in answer.

Comment on Golding's language – well done.

Excellent comments on the author's intentions.

> Golding's presentation of democracy begins in Chapter 1, when Ralph and Piggy find the conch. This object, destined to become the symbol of democratic rule, is actually a source of conflict from the start. Piggy sees it as 'valuable' but Ralph as a 'plaything'. With this contrasting language, Golding sets up the idea that the boys' attempts to use the conch to establish fair rule are just a game. It's important that Ralph is the first to wield the conch, even though it is Piggy who knows what it is. This underlines an aspect of Golding's exploration of democracy, suggesting it is only properly understood by a character who doesn't have any power. This means that from the beginning the reader will question whether the boys' experience of democracy will be positive.

Activity 9

Use one of the following question templates to write your own question around a theme – you just need to insert the theme you want to write about in the space.

- What are Golding's ideas about _____ and how does he show its different sides?

- How does Golding present the boys' experience of _____ ?

- Referring to three different parts of the novel, explain Golding's attitudes to _____ .

Activity 10

Write the opening paragraph of an answer to the question you created in Activity 9. Try to incorporate the strengths of the writing in the student answer above. Continue on separate paper if you need to.

Intertwining themes

Of course, at any single moment in the novel, multiple themes might be referenced. This means you need to read carefully and notice how Golding intertwines references to a range of ideas.

Activity 11

Read the following extract from Chapter 4 and note the different themes that Golding refers to in it. Identify where each theme is relevant in the extract by inserting arrows to key words and phrases. Then, for each theme, add a short explanation in the text boxes to explain how it is relevant at this point in the novel. Use the example given as a model.

Identity – The boys are losing their individuality, as shown by the movement away from their names to size-based labels.

Leadership

Loss of civilization

Savagery

The smaller boys were known now by the generic title of 'littluns'. The decrease in size, from Ralph down, was gradual; and though there was a dubious region inhabited by Simon and Robert and Maurice, nevertheless no one had any difficulty in recognizing biguns at one end and littluns at the other. The undoubted littluns, those aged about six, led a quite distinct, and at the same time intense, life of their own. They ate most of the day, picking fruit where they could reach it and not particular about ripeness and quality. They were used now to stomach-aches and a sort of chronic diarrhoea. They suffered untold terrors in the dark and huddled together for comfort. Apart from food and sleep, they found time for play, aimless and trivial, in the white sand by the bright water. They cried for their mothers much less often than might have been expected; they were very brown, and filthily dirty. They obeyed the summons of the conch, partly because Ralph blew it, and he was big enough to be a link with the adult world of authority; and partly because they enjoyed the entertainment of the assemblies. But otherwise they seldom bothered with the biguns and their passionately emotional and corporate life was their own.

(Chapter 4)

Fear

Loss of innocence

Democracy

Power

Activity 12

Now apply the same type of annotations as you developed in Activity 11 – naming themes and explaining their relevance – to the extract below from Chapter 8. This time, you need to identify the multiple thematic references that Golding is making on your own.

Fifteen yards from the drove Jack stopped; and his arm, straightening, pointed at the sow. He looked round in inquiry to make sure that everyone understood and the other boys nodded at him. The row of right arms slid back.

"Now!"

The drove of pigs started up; and at a range of only ten yards the wooden spears with fire-hardened points flew toward the chosen pig. One piglet, with a demented shriek, rushed into the sea trailing Roger's spear behind it. The sow gave a gasping squeal and staggered up, with two spears sticking in her fat flank. The boys shouted and rushed forward, the piglets scattered and the sow burst the advancing line and went crashing away through the forest.

"After her!"

They raced along the pig-track, but the forest was too dark and tangled so that Jack, cursing, stopped them and cast among the trees. Then he said nothing for a time but breathed fiercely so that they were awed by him and looked at each other in uneasy admiration. Presently he stabbed down at the ground with his finger.

"There—"

Before the others could examine the drop of blood, Jack had swerved off, judging a trace, touching a bough that gave. So he followed, mysteriously right and assured and the hunters trod behind him.

(Chapter 8)

Pigs

It is no coincidence, of course, that Piggy is named for the creature who becomes the focus of brutal hunting in the novel.

> **mirroring/parallels** the subtle connections between apparently distinct characters or events
>
> **simile** a technique used to compare one thing with another thing of a different kind to make a description more emphatic or vivid

Activity 13

To explore the thematic link between pigs and boys in more detail, answer the following questions.

a) 'Presently he was palely and fatly naked.' *(Chapter 1)*

Why do you think Golding chose to make Piggy intelligent, fat, pale and asthmatic?

----

b) 'One piglet, with a demented shriek, rushed into the sea trailing Roger's spear behind it…' *(Chapter 8)*

How does the treatment of this piglet **mirror** two other deaths in the novel?

----

c) 'Piggy's arms and legs twitched a bit, like a pig's after it has been killed.' *(Chapter 11)*

Why do you think Golding used this **simile** at this particular point in the novel?

----

d) Which theme do you think is explored most effectively through the **parallels** between Piggy and the hunted pigs: violence, fear, savagery – or any others? Explain your answer with references to the text.

----

e) How do the similarities between Piggy himself and pigs in the novel more generally affect the reader?

On separate paper, make a collection of all the quotations you can find in which Piggy and the pigs on the island are aligned.

Dramatic irony

Frequently, Golding uses **dramatic irony** to draw attention to key themes and ideas. This is a very effective technique as it gives the reader 'inside information'. It is especially useful in *Lord of the Flies* as Golding wants to comment on the boys' experiences without necessarily showing them as aware of the hidden meanings of their experiences.

> **dramatic irony** when the full significance of words or actions is clear to the audience or reader although unknown to the characters in the text

Activity 14

Read the two extracts from Chapter 10 and the notes on them and then answer the questions on page 74.

Ralph hit out; then he and what seemed like a dozen others were rolling over and over, hitting, biting, scratching. He was torn and jolted, found fingers in his mouth and bit them. A fist withdrew and came back like a piston, so that the whole shelter exploded into light. Ralph twisted sideways on top of a writhing body and felt hot breath on his cheek. He began to pound the mouth below him, using his clenched fist as a hammer; he hit with more and more passionate hysteria as the face became slippery. A knee jerked up between his legs and he fell sideways, busying himself with his pain, and the fight rolled over him. Then the shelter collapsed with smothering finality; and the anonymous shapes fought their way out and through. Dark figures drew themselves out of the wreckage and flitted away, till the screams of the littluns and Piggy's gasps were once more audible.

Ralph believes he is fighting the enemy but soon finds out that in fact he is attacking Eric, whose tooth he has loosened.

"I gave one of 'em what for," said Ralph, "I smashed him up all right. He won't want to come and fight us again in a hurry."

"So did I," said Eric. "When I woke up one was kicking me in the face. I got an awful bloody face, I think, Ralph. But I did him in the end."

"What did you do?"

"I got my knee up," said Eric with simple pride, "and I hit him with it in the pills. You should have heard him holler! He won't come back in a hurry either. So we didn't do too badly."

Ralph moved suddenly in the dark; but then he heard Eric working at his mouth.

"What's the matter?"

"Jus' a tooth loose."

Eric thinks he hit one of the enemy camp between the legs, but in fact it was Ralph who was on the other end of this attack.

a) How do Ralph and Eric's mistakes affect you as a reader? Do you find them amusing, tragic or shocking? Explain your answer fully.

b) What is happening to Piggy while Ralph and Eric are mistakenly fighting each other? (You may need to read the end of the Chapter 10 to remind yourself.)

c) Thinking about the theme of innate evil and Simon's revelation that 'the beast' stands for this, why do you think Golding included this moment of dramatic irony?

Progress check

Use the chart below to review the skills you have developed in this chapter.
For each column, start at the bottom box and work your way up towards the
highest level in the top box. Tick the box to show you have achieved that level.

I can sustain a critical response to *Lord of the Flies* and interpret the themes convincingly ☐	I use a wide range of vocabulary and can spell and punctuate consistently and accurately ☐
I can develop a coherent response to *Lord of the Flies* and explain the themes clearly ☐	I use a range of vocabulary and can spell and punctuate, mostly accurately ☐
I can make some comments on the themes in *Lord of the Flies* ☐	I use a simple range of vocabulary and spell and punctuate with some accuracy ☐
Personal response	**Technical accuracy**

Understanding questions

Doing your best in any exam is all about preparation. After your close reading of *Lord of the Flies* and working through this book, you should be feeling confident about the sorts of things you will write about. In this section, you will get ready for different sorts of exam questions, practise writing answers and review sample responses that you can learn from.

Activity 1

Complete the table below by formulating another example question using each key question word. You will find some exam question words that crop up again and again.

Key exam question word	What do you have to do?	Example question	Your own example question
Explore	Investigate openly and write about a range of different ideas.	Explore the role of Roger in the novel as a whole.	
Explain	Put forward different views, with reasons to justify them.	Explain the importance of the island in the novel.	
In what ways	Present a range of ideas and explain them.	In what ways is Jack and Ralph's relationship significant?	
How far/To what extent	Evaluate the level or amount of something.	To what extent can anyone be blamed for Simon's death?	
How does Golding	Examine the techniques the author uses.	How does Golding create tension in this extract?	

Making up your own questions and writing essay plans and whole answers is a great revision activity. Try to do this more as you get closer to the exam, setting yourself the same time limit you will have in the exam.

In the exam, avoid launching straight into writing your answer. Make sure you really understand what the question is asking. Pay attention to the key question words and remind yourself what they mean. Turning the exam question into a mini spider diagram is a good way to help you focus on what is being asked and to start planning. Here is an example.

Need to mention a number of ways – could think about what they each stand for, as well as how their relationship changes.

Focus on Piggy and Ralph's relationship – could use beginning of novel, talk about conch, rescue plan and fire (NB Piggy's glasses), Piggy being different class, Ralph depending on Piggy, both rejected by Jack, how Ralph feels when Piggy dies.

In what way is Piggy and Ralph's relationship significant?

This could mean significant to plot as well as ideas. Ralph and Piggy start the novel and Ralph's last thoughts when rescue comes are about him. But also significant because Piggy stands for intelligence, Ralph for democracy.

Activity 2

Using the example above as a guide, explore each of these possible exam questions with mini spider diagrams.

How does Golding present Jack as a leader in the novel?

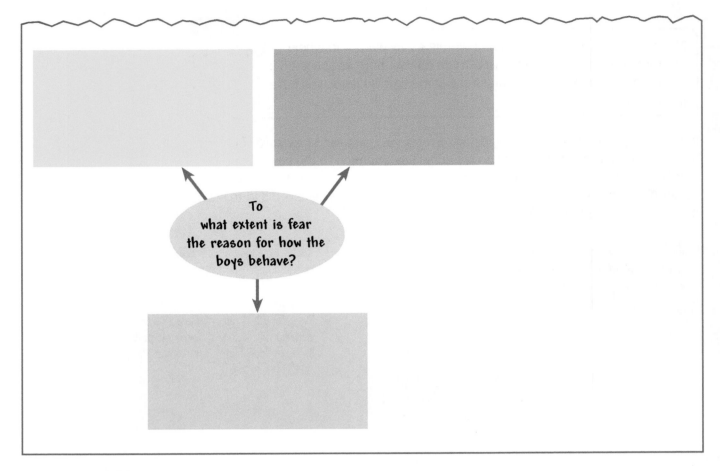

To what extent is fear the reason for how the boys behave?

Exam techniques

Sometimes things go wrong in exams. This is not surprising, because people are under pressure and it is easy to make mistakes. But being well prepared includes understanding good exam techniques. For example, you should:

- read the question at least three times
- use some of the time allowed to plan your answer – and do not cross it out, as you may be given credit for things you have included in your plan
- make sure your grammar, punctuation and spelling are the best they can be – there are some marks for this
- answer the question!

This last piece of advice sounds so obvious and yet every year, many students go wrong by not answering the question – make sure you read the exam instructions and the question carefully and keep checking as you write each paragraph of your answer that it is focused on the question.

Getting started

Activity 3

Four students are in a panic as their exam starts and they are each about to make a classic mistake.

Rewrite the beginning of answers a-c for the students, using the student 1 answer as a model.

Student 1 is answering the question 'Explore the role of Piggy in the novel as a whole.'

And thinking about starting with…

> Lord of the Flies is an allegorical adventure story set on an island with a range of characters who represent different ideas about power and evil…

Stop! You haven't got to write everything you know about *Lord of the Flies* in this exam. Focus on the question.

A better start is…

Piggy is established as an important character at the novel's opening. We meet him

second after Ralph and within a few pages his intelligence has been demonstrated by his

identification of the conch.

a) Student 2 is answering the question 'Explain the importance of three different island locations in the novel.'

And thinking about starting with…

> Lord of the Flies is set on a tropical island. When the boys' plane crashes, a scar is made. Soon the boys start to use a platform of rock as a meeting place…

Stop! You are retelling the story. Use your first sentence to make a clear case for the three locations you are going to choose.

A better start is…

----

b) Student 3 is answering the question 'How effective do you find the end of the novel?'

And thinking about starting with...

> In this essay I am going to write about the end of the novel and whether I think it is effective. I will consider whether it is realistic and if Golding could have written a different ending.

Stop! You are wasting time and words. Never begin an essay with 'In this essay I am going to...' – just get on with the answer.

A better start is...

----

c) Student 4 is answering the question 'To what extent do the boys enjoy violence in *Lord of the Flies*?'

And thinking about starting with...

> William Golding, the author of Lord of the Flies, was born in 1911 and fought in the Second World War. He was also a teacher and a father of boys. Lord of the Flies was published in...

Stop! Some of this contextual information might be relevant to the presentation of violence in the novel, but include it as you go along. Make sure your first paragraph starts actually to answer the question.

A better start is...

Exam requirements

Exams vary, as do the tasks you have to do on set books. Knowing the text as well as possible is the best way to get ready for whatever challenges you will face, but you should also find out as much as you can about the way in which you are going to be tested.

Activity 4

Carry out some research to find out the answers to the questions below. You can do this by:

- asking your teachers
- studying examples of relevant exam papers or past questions
- looking at the website of the exam board that runs your exam or coursework.

a) How much time in total will you have to read the text and get ready?

---

b) How long will you have to write your answer on *Lord of the Flies*?

---

c) Will you have to answer an open essay-style question or a question based on an extract from the novel?

---

d) Will you be allowed to have a copy of the novel with you when you are writing?

---

e) How many marks are available for the question on *Lord of the Flies* and what percentage of the total marks is this?

However you are being tested, you need to show that you have:

- an understanding of the themes and ideas of the novel
- an insight into and perception of less obvious meanings
- an ability to choose relevant evidence and apt quotations to back up points
- an appreciation of Golding's techniques and their effect on the reader
- a clear and fluent way of writing about your ideas
- a good vocabulary, accurate spelling, grammar and punctuation.

Activity 5

a) Put the items from the list above into the following table, ranking them from 'most challenging' (10) to 'least challenging' (0). Remember that your finished list may not be the same as anyone else's because everyone has their own strengths and weaknesses.

Exam requirements	Level of challenge for me
	10
	0

b) Focus on the two things that you ranked the highest level of challenge and therefore feel least confident about. Write two action points for each. These should be things you can do before the exam to improve your confidence.

For example, if you feel that 'understanding the themes and ideas of the novel' is a weakness for you, you could decide to:

  i. work through the 'Themes' chapter of this book again

    and

  ii. make a revision card for each main theme, including an explanation in your own words and three key quotations.

Close reading skills

Remember that, whatever the question, showing off your close reading skills is your best chance of doing well. This means you need to:

- remember the main plot events and how they relate to each other
- consider how characters change and develop during the novel
- pay attention to Golding's language choices and their effect
- link plot, characters and language to themes and ideas.

Activity 6

Practise bringing all your reading skills and understanding together by reading the extract below from Chapter 3 and answering the questions on pages 84–5. Annotate the extract to help you answer the questions.

> Jack was bent double. He was down like a sprinter, his nose only a few inches from the humid earth. The tree trunks and the creepers that festooned them lost themselves in a green dusk thirty feet above him; and all about was the undergrowth. There was only the faintest indication of a trail here; a cracked twig and what might be the impression of one side of a hoof. He lowered his chin and stared at the traces as though he would force them to speak to him. Then dog-like, uncomfortably on all fours yet unheeding his discomfort, he stole forward five yards and stopped. Here was a loop of creeper with a tendril pendant from a node. The tendril was polished on the under-side; pigs, passing through the loop, brushed it with their bristly hide.
>
> Jack crouched with his face a few inches away from this clue, then stared forward into the semi-darkness of the undergrowth. His sandy hair, considerably longer than it had been when they dropped in, was lighter now; and his bare back was a mass of dark freckles and peeling sunburn. A sharpened stick about five feet long trailed from his right hand; and except for a pair of tattered shorts held up by his knife-belt he was naked. He closed his eyes, raised his head and breathed in gently with flared nostrils, assessing the current of warm air for information. The forest and he were very still.
>
> *(Chapter 3)*

a) According to this extract, in what physical ways has Jack changed since the beginning of the novel?

----

b) 'Like a sprinter', 'dog-like': what impression of Jack do we get from these similes?

----

c) Find three phrases that show Jack's relationship with the jungle setting at this point, and explain your choices.

----

d) This extract is from the beginning of Chapter 3. How does the first simple sentence introduce it? Why is the last sentence of the extract important?

----

e) How far do you think Jack has gone on his journey towards savagery?

----

f) What does Golding want us to think about the idea of savagery at this stage?

Planning

Here are three essay questions that refer to the extract on page 83.

a) According to this extract, in what physical ways has Jack changed since the beginning of the novel?

b) Explore the way Golding presents the island at the beginning of Chapter 3 and at two other times in the novel.

c) With reference to the beginning of Chapter 3 and any other relevant part of the novel, show how Golding explores the idea of the boys' descent from civilization to savagery.

Activity 7

Using the ideas you came up with in Activity 6 and any other relevant points, complete the following flow diagram style plan for question a above.

a) According to this extract, in what physical ways has Jack changed since the beginning of the novel?

> Opening paragraph – state that Golding presents Jack's journey towards being a savage quite gradually and explain. I will look at his first appearance on the beach, the beginning of Chapter 3 and the first pig-killing.

↓

> Brief account of Jack's first appearance. Contrast with other boys. Leader of choir. Jack's power. Golding gives us clues that Jack will become more of a threat later. Affects me by being bossy and menacing.

↓

> ---
> ---
> ---

↓

> ---
> ---
> ---

Conclude by summing up how Jack changes and what I think of him. Link to themes of savagery and power. Golding uses Jack to represent how easy it is for veneer of civilized good behaviour to rub off in difficult circumstances. End on question – is Jack truly evil or a victim of circumstances?

Activity 8

Choose either question b or c from the questions on the previous page and create a spider diagram essay plan to show how you would respond in the exam. Aim for five main, well-developed points and a concluding paragraph.

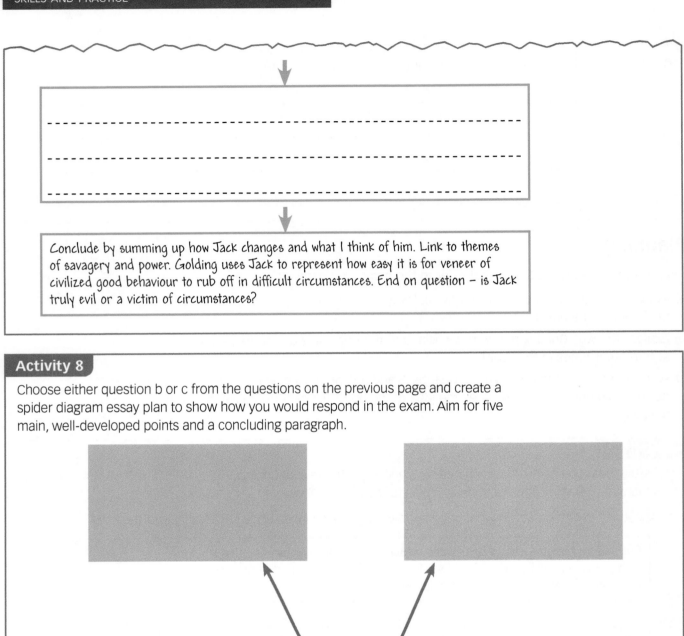

Activity 9

Read the following extract from Chapter 7 and the example questions a–d on page 88. Circle the question you would answer and complete the chart plan to show how you would answer it. Annotate the extract to help with your planning.

All at once, Robert was screaming and struggling with the strength of frenzy. Jack had him by the hair and was brandishing his knife. Behind him was Roger, fighting to get close. The chant rose ritually, as at the last moment of a dance or a hunt.

"Kill the pig! Cut his throat! Kill the pig! Bash him in!"

Ralph too was fighting to get near, to get a handful of that brown, vulnerable flesh. The desire to squeeze and hurt was over-mastering.

Jack's arm came down; the heaving circle cheered and made pig-dying noises. Then they lay quiet, panting, listening to Robert's frightened snivels. He wiped his face with a dirty arm, and made an effort to retrieve his status.

"Oh, my bum!"

He rubbed his rump ruefully. Jack rolled over.

"That was a good game."

"Just a game," said Ralph uneasily. "I got jolly badly hurt at rugger once."

"We ought to have a drum," said Maurice, "then we could do it properly."

Ralph looked at him.

"How properly?"

"I dunno. You want a fire, I think, and a drum, and you keep time to the drum."

"You want a pig," said Roger, "like a real hunt."

"Or someone to pretend," said Jack. "You could get someone to dress up as a pig and then he could act – you know, pretend to knock me over and all that – "

"You want a real pig," said Robert, still caressing his rump, "because you've got to kill him."

"Use a littlun," said Jack, and everybody laughed.

(Chapter 7)

a) Look at the extract from Chapter 7. How does the extract highlight the themes of the novel as a whole?

b) Using this extract as a starting point, explore the way Golding uses hunting in the novel to show the boys' characters and personalities.

c) To what extent is this a significant moment in the novel?

d) "That was a good game," says Jack. Explain the importance of games in the novel.

Opening paragraph

-
-
-

Paragraph 1	Paragraph 2	Paragraph 3	Paragraph 4
•	•	•	•
•	•	•	•
•	•	•	•

Concluding paragraph

-
-
-

Practice

Activity 10

This student chose question c. Read the answer below, then match the feedback comments (a–e) to the numbered points in the text and respond to the marker's questions and prompts.

C) To what extent is this a significant moment in the novel?

At first glance this may not seem like a very important moment because it is quite short, not all the characters are there and it is just about a game being played. On the other hand, it is important because it highlights a number of themes and displays some of the personalities of the key characters. [1]

The moment is a play-hunt that takes place during a real hunt. It shows that the boys are still boys, even though things on the island are getting harder. In the previous chapter, Sam and Eric reported that they have seen 'the beast' and a group, led by Jack, have gone off to find it. [2]

Another reason the moment is important is because of what it shows about Ralph. This is one of the first times that 'Ralph was content to follow Jack.' This is ominous because it is a warning about when Jack completely takes over by the end. In the extract it says that the 'desire to squeeze and hurt was over-mastering', so Ralph seems to be letting his inner wildness and savagery take over. Golding puts us inside Ralph's head so we can see how he sees Robert as 'brown, vulnerable flesh' – not even human. But just before this moment, Ralph has been remembering his home and 'the books' so he is not completely savage. Also, Ralph is still uncomfortable about the violence. We can see this when he repeats the idea of the hunt just being 'a game' and compares it to rugby. Maybe Golding is showing that Ralph's top layer of civilization is wearing off.

a It is good to mention 'the beast' but do not just tell the story. Make a link between the deeper meaning of the beast, representing the evil inside the boys, and this moment.

b This introduction is too vague – make it more precise by saying which themes and character traits the moment highlights.

Thinking about what happens to Piggy and Simon also shows that this moment is important. Although Robert is not killed, he is terrified, 'screaming and struggling with the strength of frenzy'. Then he tries to show that he is not bothered by making a joke about his 'bum'. The boys do not seem to recognize the importance of the scene and the way they have been treating Robert. [3]

As expected, Jack leads the attack on Robert and Roger is just 'behind him'. Maurice is also involved, which reminds me of when he and Roger kicked the sandcastles down. Then, Roger threw stones at one of the others but Maurice did not because he remembered being told off about it. At this moment though, it is like [4] Maurice has forgotten about being told off for hurting people. Golding is showing that the boys are forgetting the adult world.

Another reason this extract is important is because of how the boys use the play-hunt as a preparation for a real hunt. The chanting is the same chanting as they use later when Simon dies. This is an effective way to link the pretend hunt to the real one that does end in a death. At this stage, the boys think that doing things 'properly' is having a drum and keeping time. Even when Robert reminds everyone that you are supposed to kill the pig at the end, it is as if they are still talking about a game because 'everyone laughed'. For the reader this is not funny – at least one littlun has already disappeared because the older ones did not take responsibility, and now they are making a joke out of killing another one.

Overall, I think the extract is important because it raises the theme of savagery and foreshadows the death of Simon. [5]

c A good final point – develop with an extra sentence about Simon's death and what it shows about the boys.

d Avoid colloquial language in an essay. Rewrite this more formally. You could phrases such as 'it suggests' or 'this gives the impression'.

e Agreed – the boys dismiss the scene as a game. However, the reader sees things differently. Say more about how Golding uses dramatic irony here.

Activity 11

Read this further sample answer to a different question on *Lord of the Flies*.

> `All the boys start good and end up evil.´
>
> How far do you agree with this comment on *Lord of the Flies*?

The first character that Golding introduces is Ralph and at first sight he seems 'good'. He takes a childish delight in the island and has no embarrassment or anxiety – he quickly strips off to swim, 'in the middle of the scar he stood on his head' and he pretends to be a fighter plane even though he has just experienced a horrific crash. This suggests his innocent and carefree attitude, like Adam and Eve in the Bible story about the Garden of Eden. But even from this early point, Ralph has a darker side. Maybe it is not presented as evil at this stage, but Ralph does seem to judge Piggy, he does not ask his name and he is quick to make fun of him – "sucks to your ass-mar!"

Piggy, on the other hand, is a more straightforward character. He wants to make friends with Ralph, and he seems harmless and kind, for example, when he gathers the younger children. He thinks things through and wants to improve island life – "we could make a sundial" – and he is rational, refusing to believe in ghosts or 'the beast'. This makes him seem sensible. I think Golding also associates Piggy with the outside world – his glasses are the way the boys can make fire-smoke, and smoke is the only way they can be rescued. The conch – which he identified in Chapter 1 – could also be a sign of his goodness. On the other hand, Golding shows Piggy as weak – he does not remember the name of the boy who goes missing, and he does not have any leadership skills. Perhaps Golding is saying Piggy is good, but being good is not enough. Piggy does not turn evil, though.

In a way, all the boys have a good and bad side. In my view, there is only one exception to this: Simon. Simon represents pure goodness, and he is a complete outsider because of it. His first act in the novel is to faint – this makes him seem delicate and not able to cope with life on the island. But actually he has a very positive link with the nature on the island – he recognizes the plants and 'wormed his way' into the heart of the jungle. In many of his scenes, Simon is linked to butterflies, which could also be a symbol of his innocence. Simon also has other qualities that we think of as being good; he is loyal, he is hard-working (he helps Ralph with the shelters) and he is kind (he gets the littluns fruit when they can not reach it). Some people say that Simon represents Christ, especially because he goes off into the forest on his own and because he is the one that understands that the boys are the evil thing on the island. It is ironic that he is killed when he is bringing the boys the message that the beast was harmless. Simon does not end up evil. Perhaps Golding is saying that he is too good to survive. But if Simon were truly good, would he not stand up to Jack and Roger? Golding seems to be saying that goodness on its own is not enough – you have to have power.

Jack does have power, but at the beginning of the book he does not seem evil, just bossy. Although, from the very beginning Golding presents him with a warning, because he is the leader of the 'black, bat-like creature' that turns out to be the choir. Jack does seem to lose his civilized ways more easily than some of the others – he is the first, for example, to paint his face, and he leads the hunting. I think Golding is putting over the idea that some people are more able to become evil than others. Roger is another example of a character who has less good in him and becomes more evil. Although he is the one who suggests "let's have a vote", by the end of the novel he has a 'stick sharpened at both ends', which is a symbol of horrible cruelty.

On the beach in the final scene, we see Ralph again, crying 'for the end of innocence'. This suggests that by the end of the novel Ralph is still good. He is not perfect and he has performed some evil acts – he took part in the murder of Simon – but he does not end up evil. Maybe this is because Golding wanted to show that there was some hope, or maybe it is just because he wanted Ralph to be the character that had too much goodness for it to be totally lost. In either case, although several of the boys do seem to end up showing their evil side, Ralph does not.

a) Identify the strengths of this student's writing by completing the second column of the table below to show how this answer meets the exam criteria.

Successful answers show...	Example from this sample answer for each aspect	Example from your own practice answer for each aspect
Understanding of the themes and ideas of the novel		
Insight and perception about less obvious meanings		
Ability to choose relevant evidence and apt quotations to back up points		

Appreciation of Golding's techniques and their effect on the reader		
A clear and fluent way of writing about ideas		
Good vocabulary, accurate spelling, grammar and punctuation		

b) Write your own practice answer to one of these two questions in your notebook and use the third column in the table to check that you have included all the features of a successful answer.

   i. In what ways is *Lord of the Flies* a successful adventure story?

   ii. Explain the importance of leadership in the novel.

Progress check

Use the chart below to review the skills you have developed in this chapter.
For each column, start at the bottom box and work your way up towards the
highest level in the top box. Tick the box to show you have achieved that level.

I can use well-integrated textual references from *Lord of the Flies* to support my interpretation ☐	I use a wide range of vocabulary and can spell and punctuate consistently and accurately ☐
I can use quotations and other textual references from *Lord of the Flies* to support my explanation ☐	I use a range of vocabulary and can spell and punctuate, mostly accurately ☐
I can make references to some details from *Lord of the Flies* ☐	I use a simple range of vocabulary and spell and punctuate with some accuracy ☐
Textual references	**Technical accuracy**

Glossary

allegory   a story with a hidden meaning in which characters, events and objects have a symbolic function

characterization   the ways that fictional characters are created or constructed

chronologically   in time order, beginning with the earliest

class   ordering of society where people are divided into sets based on perceived social or economic status

climax   a significant moment when things go wrong

context   the circumstances that form the setting for a piece of literature and can help readers to understand it

denouement   the final part of a novel when the various strands of the plot are brought together and resolved.

dramatic irony   when the full significance of words or actions is clear to the audience or reader although unknown to the characters in the text

exposition   an introdction where the scene is set for the drama to follow

falling action   when the conflict starts to be resolved but there is continued drama or suspense

foreshadowing   when an author gives clues, warnings and indications about future events

internal monologue   when the reader feels as though they are inside a character's head because their thoughts are presented directly (without 'he said' or 'he thought')

juxtaposition   placing two opposite ideas or meanings near or next to each other to draw attention to the similarities or contrasts between them

mirroring/parallels   the subtle connections between apparently distinct characters or events

narrative voice   the voice used to tell the story

omniscient narrator   a narrator who knows everything about the characters, including inner thoughts and feelings

pathetic fallacy   a literary technique that gives human qualities or emotions to inanimate objects of nature; for example, when weather is used to reflect a particular mood

personification   a type of metaphor where human qualities are given to objects or ideas

plot   the main events of a play, novel, film, or similar work, presented by the writer as an interrelated sequence

rising action   a series of problems or conflicts that increase the tension

simile   a technique used to compare one thing with another thing of a different kind to make a description more emphatic or vivid

structure   the way a text develops across its parts

symbol   a thing that represents or stands for something else

theme   an idea that recurs in a work of literature

third person   from the point of view of a character using the pronouns 'he' or 'she' (as opposed to first person, which uses the pronoun 'I')

tragedy   a traditional story type with five main stages, first defined by the Ancient Greek philosopher and scientist Aristotle

Great Clarendon Street, Oxford, OX2 6DP, United Kingdom

Oxford University Press is a department of the University of Oxford.
It furthers the University's objective of excellence in research, scholarship,
and education by publishing worldwide. Oxford is a registered trade mark
of Oxford University Press in the UK and in certain other countries

British Library Cataloguing in Publication Data

Data available

ISBN 978-019-839890-5

10 9 8 7 6 5 4 3 2

Printed in Great Britain by CPI Group (UK) Ltd., Croydon CR0 4YY

Acknowledgements

We are grateful for permission to reprint the following copyright material:

William Golding: extracts from *Lord of the Flies* (Faber, 1997), reprinted by
permission of the publishers, Faber & Faber Ltd.

The author and the publisher would also like to thank the following for
permission to reproduce material:

Cover: Penny Tweedie/Alamy Stock Photo